KEITH URBAN
Love, Pain & the whole crazy thing

CONTENTS

This book was approved by Keith Urban

Cover photography by Max Vadukul

Transcribed by Jeff Jacobson

Cherry Lane Music Company
Director of Publications/Project Editor: Mark Phillips
Manager of Publications: Gabrielle Fastman

ISBN-13: 978-1-57560-957-7
ISBN-10: 1-57560-957-6

Visit our website at www.cherrylane.com

KEITH URBAN
Love, Pain & the whole crazy thing

albums from 1999's *Keith Urban*, to 2002's *Golden Road*, to 2004's *Be Here*, which topped Billboard's Top Country Album charts as well as hit number three on the Billboard 200. *Keith Urban* and *Golden Road*, combined, produced seven Top 5 singles, including four number ones with sales of more than four million. Ultimately, *Be Here*, which went platinum in every country in which it was released, and four times platinum in the United States, would yield five smash singles ("Days Go By," "You're My Better Half," "Better Life," "Making Memories Of Us," and "Tonight I Wanna Cry"). Urban earned his first Grammy Award for Best Male Country Performance and the very prestigious Entertainer of the Year Award from the Country Music Association.

Anyone who imagined that the massive success of *Be Here* and the flurry of honors that followed it would lead Urban to rest on his laurels is in for a big, bold, and rather beautiful surprise.

Love, Pain & the whole crazy thing, a multi-textured work, which Urban co-produced with longtime collaborator Dann Huff, is already being lauded as the most ambitious, accomplished, and intimate album in Urban's already impressive career.

Of *Love, Pain & the whole crazy thing*, Urban says, "It's just an accurate reflection of where I am now. I think it's the sound of being happy with my life and passionate about the music that I'm making." As for the album's intriguing title, Urban explains, "It's inspired by a great old movie called *Love and Pain and the Whole Damn Thing*. We just swapped the 'Damn' for 'Crazy' and it gave the right sense of how the album feels and what it's all about. It's about Love, Pain and the Whole Crazy Thing. It's about life. When

Nearly a decade and a half after he first came to America from Australia, Keith Urban has arrived in a major way as a global musical force. This accomplished singer/songwriter and multi-instrumentalist has slowly but surely established himself as one of the most consistent and exciting talents not simply in county music, but in our music world as a whole.

A sense of steady artistic growth has been apparent since Urban's American debut as part of the country rock trio The Ranch back in 1997. There's been a series of increasingly acclaimed solo the title came to me, it was obvious—it seemed to fit."

Recorded and written with key collaborators from previous recordings, including producer Dann Huff and engineer Justin Niebank, *Love, Pain & the whole crazy thing* seems set to generate another string of hit songs. Yet each and every one of them feels exceptionally fresh.

As Urban explains, "It's a lot of the same team as the last two records, but in a way it seems quite a bit on from the last record. I think it's because there is a sense of a feeling of a full heart here—so much so that just playing music these days feels different to me. There is much more of a balance to my life—and to my music—than there has been in the past. If this album is reflective of anything, it's reflective of the peace that I feel now and the desire I have to keep reaching to try different things."

That sense of overflowing passion is at the heart of who Keith Urban is today. "I don't think back too much because I'm so focused on the now and on the future. I think of myself as a work in progress, so I'm always moving forward by my nature. I'm just grateful that I have the freedom to go and make the record that I've just made—big kudos to Capitol Records for believing in me and supporting that freedom."

Of his vision for the album, Urban explains, "What I try to make are records that have an ebb and flow, that you can listen to from top to bottom and that take you on a journey. The result is a record with a lot of diversity. It was also great to play a few more instruments this time around. For instance, when it comes to piano playing, I'm not an accomplished pianist, but that was the appeal of it for me—the texture without the technique."

With Urban and Dann Huff producing, the album has no shortage of textures. "Dann's got a great sense of arrangement, and he's really gotten to know me after three records. He knows when to push and when to back off. He's also very creative in the studio, so I take more creative risks because I trust him."

Also making a major contribution to the album is David Campbell, who was responsible for the string arrangements and an unlikely choir arrangement that graces the introduction for "God Made Woman." For Urban, "It was fantastic with David. He's got a great quirky bent, but he also understands the majestic approach to string arrangements."

One other notable guest is Ronnie Dunn of country superstars Brooks & Dunn, who appears on "Raise The Barn," an uplifting salute to those rebuilding in the wake of Hurricane Katrina. "I've always wanted to do a song with Ronnie and, strangely enough, he records all of his vocals in this old barn on his property. Needless to say, when we did it there was a whole lot of 'raising' going on."

As far as songwriting is concerned, *Love, Pain & the whole crazy thing* reflects a prolific time in Urban's career. "I found this house in Nashville that had a great room in the front of it, with windows all around and amazing views, where I could set up my studio. It was supposed to be the dining room, but I sacrificed that for the music. I just had the feeling I could write a lot of songs in that environment, and as it turned out, almost all of the songs for this album were written there."

Now Urban is ready to bring the songs to life onstage. "With the album completed, I can now see how there might have been something subconsciously at work in the creation of these songs. I think in the arena environment that we've been fortunate to find ourselves in, these songs are going to feel very much at home."

Asked if he's proud to be bringing so many people into the large world of country music, Keith Urban says, "If what I do encourages people to discover country music, including artists that I grew up listening to, then I'm grateful for the opportunity. I see it as a diverse genre, from the traditional to the contemporary. The point is that there is a lot of great music of all sorts out there to discover."

Ultimately, though, Urban's musical mission with *Love, Pain & the whole crazy thing* is much more personal than that. "I just want to be true to my music and share it," he explains. "I hope I've done that."

Once In A Lifetime

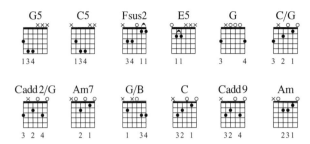

Words and Music by
Keith Urban and John Shanks

Intro
Moderately ♩ = 136

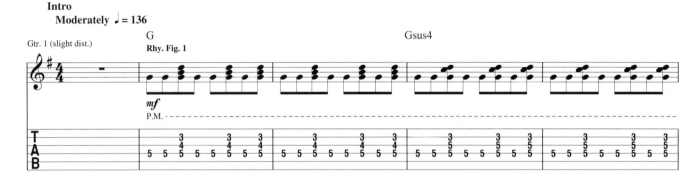

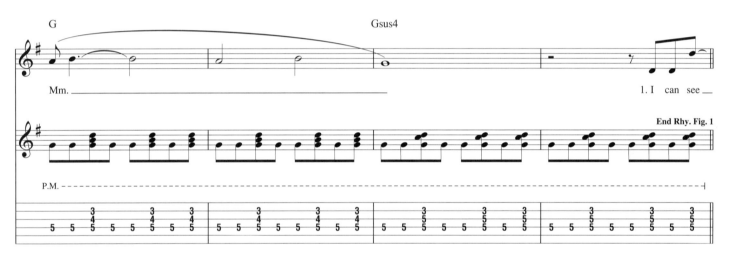

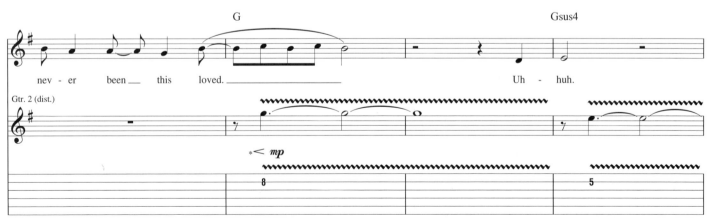

*Vol. swell

*Chord symbols reflect overall harmony.

𝄋 Pre-Chorus

2nd time, Gtr. 1: w/ Riff D (8 times)
2nd time, Gtr. 4 tacet (next 6 meas.)
2nd time, Gtrs. 7 & 8 tacet

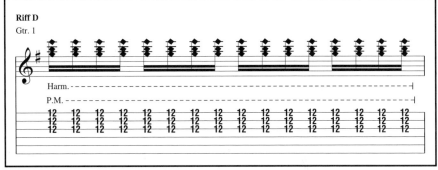

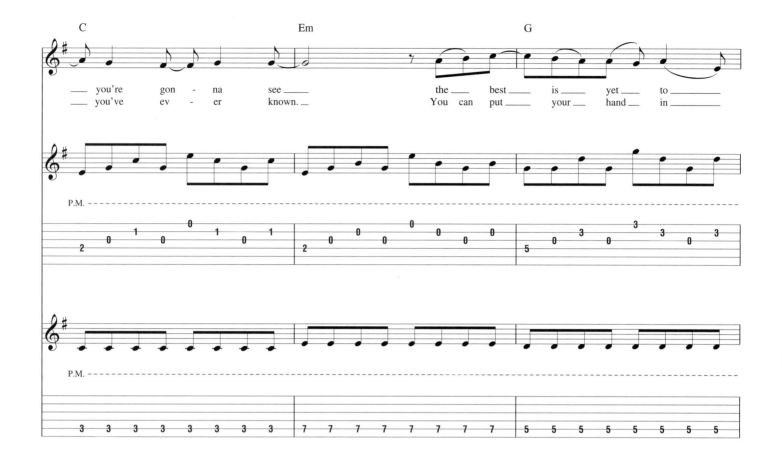

you're   gon - na   see ___   the ___ best ___ is ___ yet   to ___
you've   ev - er   known. ___   You   can   put ___   your ___ hand ___ in ___

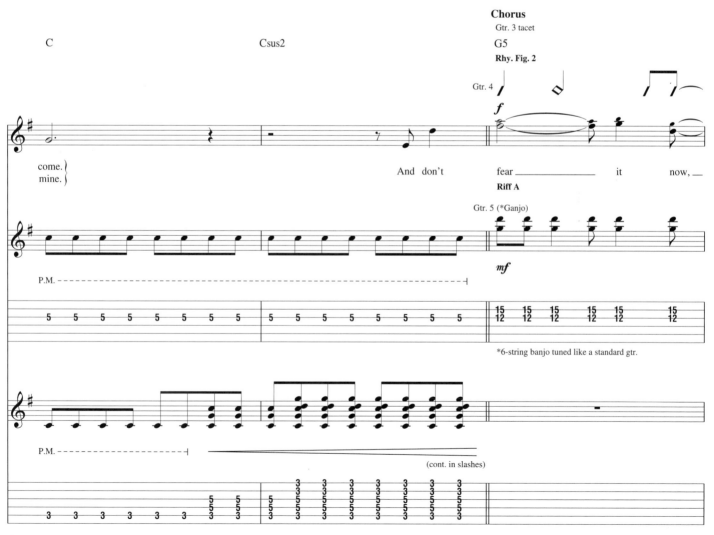

Chorus
Gtr. 3 tacet

Rhy. Fig. 2

Gtr. 4

come.⎫
mine.⎭   And   don't   fear _____   it   now, ___

Riff A

Gtr. 5 (*Ganjo)

*6-string banjo tuned like a standard gtr.

(cont. in slashes)

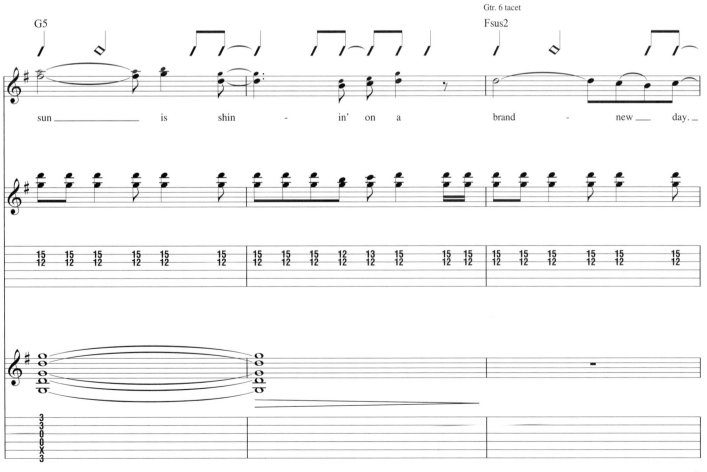

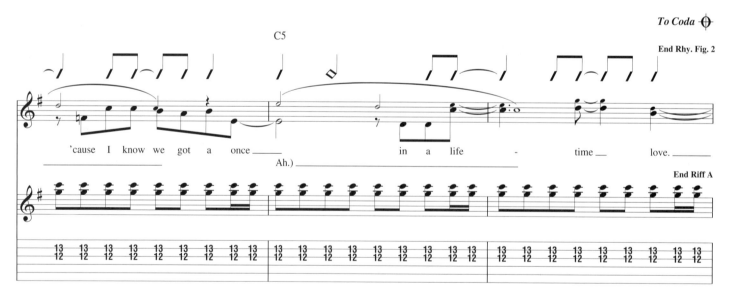

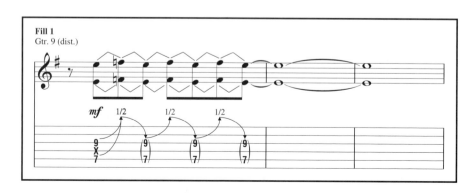

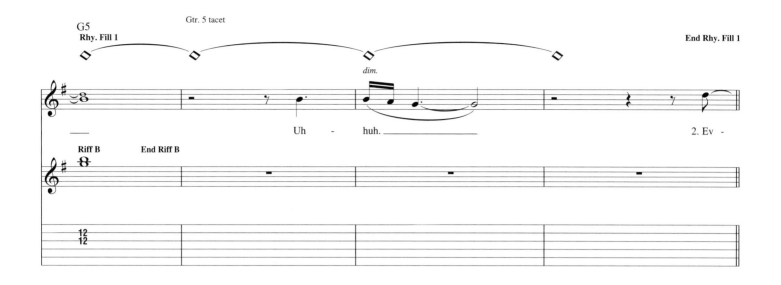

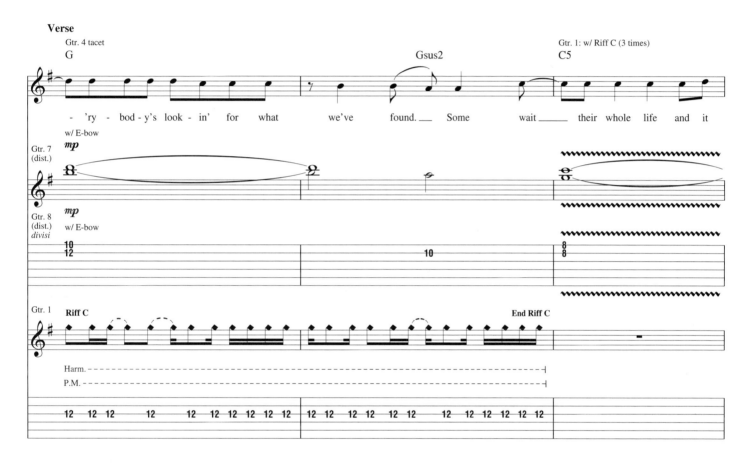

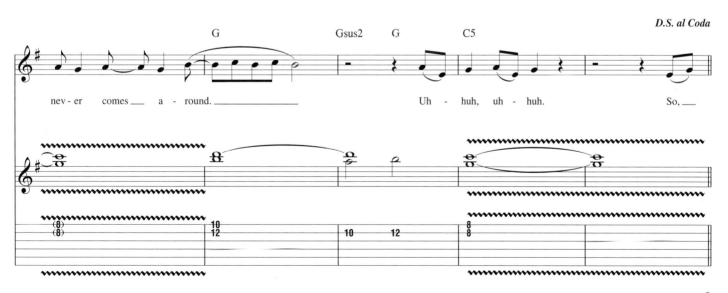

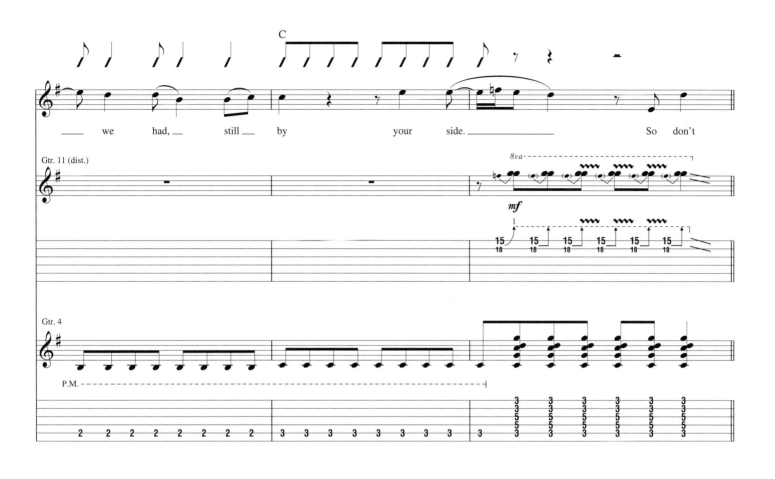

we had, still by your side. So don't

Chorus
Gtr. 4: w/ Rhy. Fig. 2 (1st 12 meas.)
Gtr. 5: w/ Riff A (1st 14 meas.)
Gtr. 10 tacet

fear it now, we're go-in' all the way.

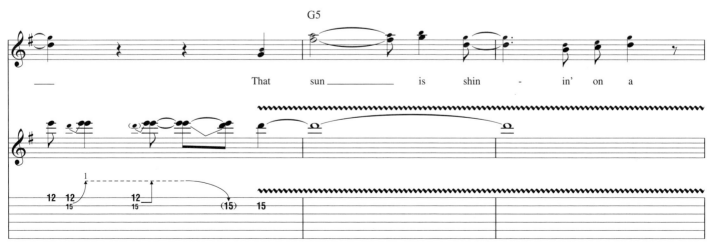

That sun is shin-in' on a

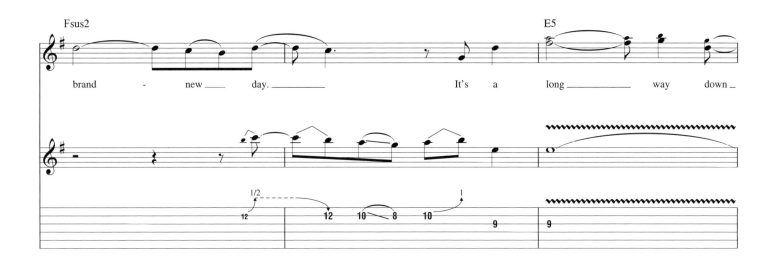

brand - new ___ day. ___ It's a long ___ way down ___

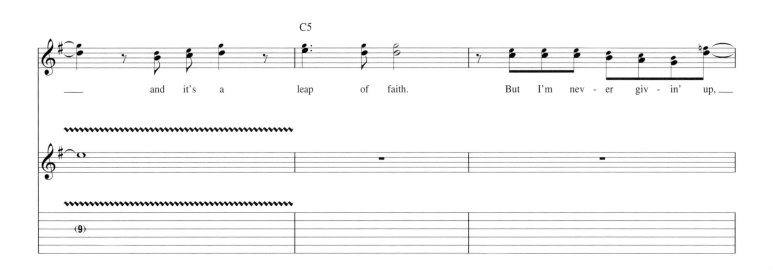

___ and it's a leap of faith. But I'm nev - er giv - in' up, ___

Gtr. 5: w/ Riff A

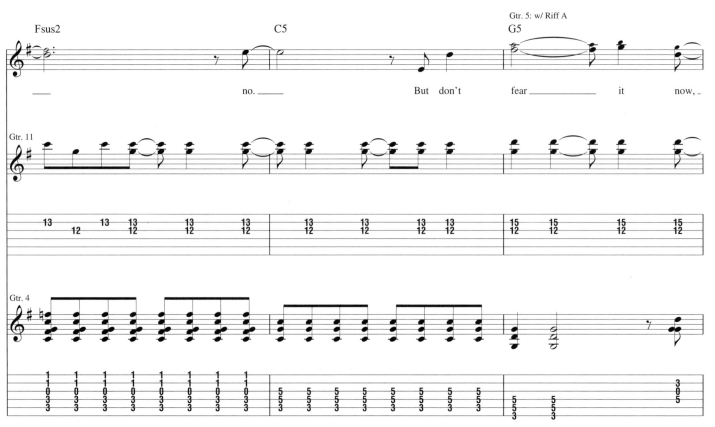

___ no. ___ But don't fear ___ it now, _

Gtr. 11

Gtr. 4

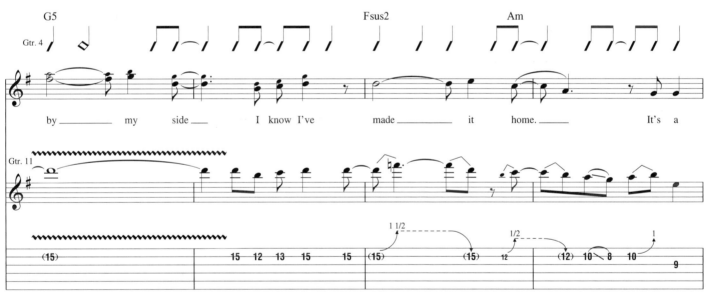

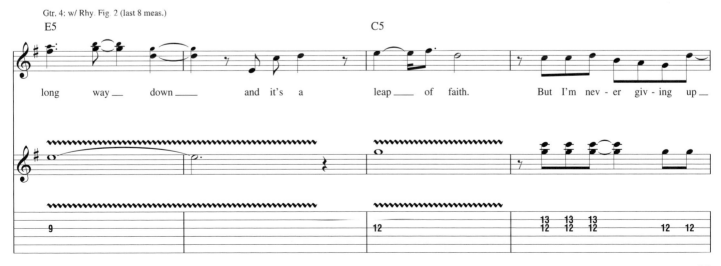

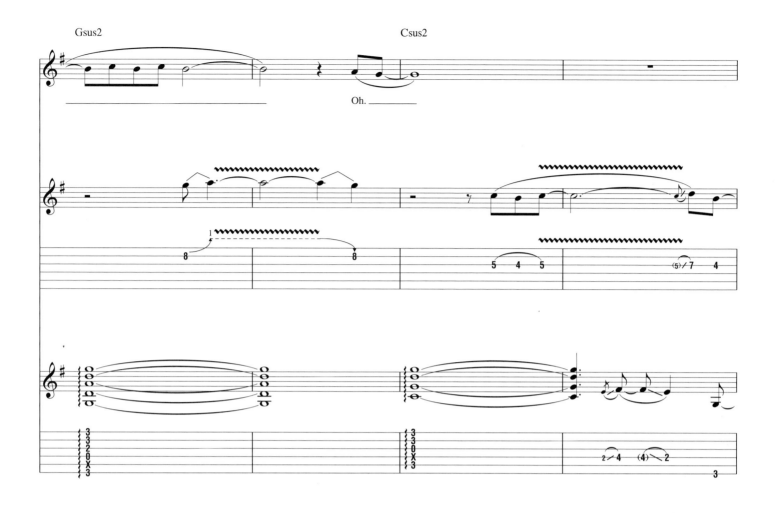

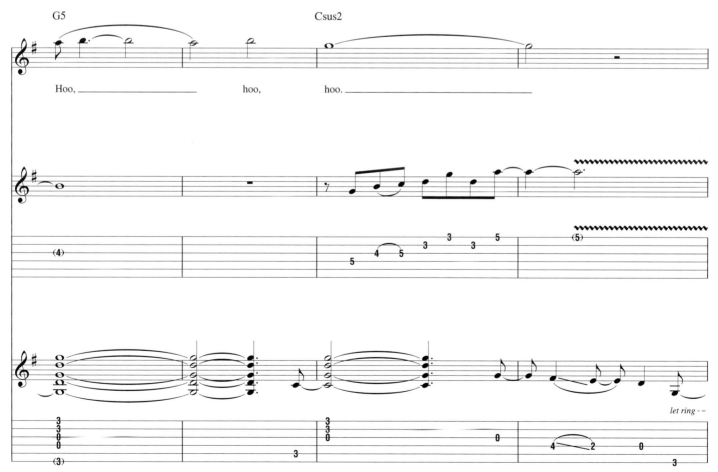

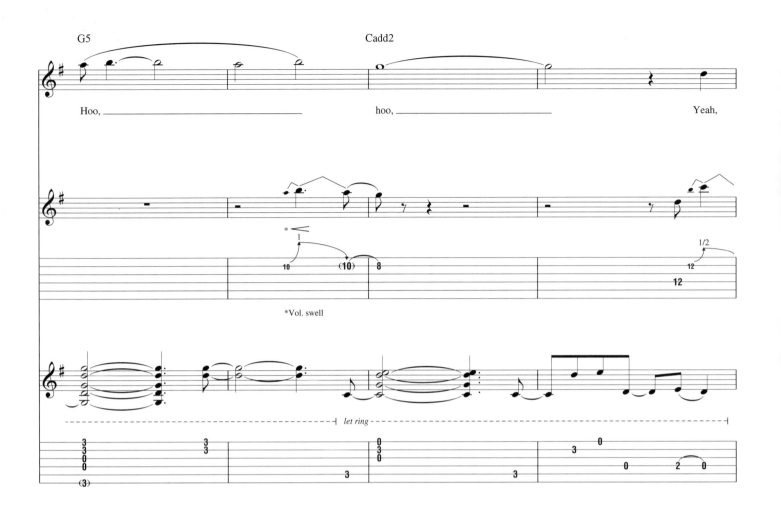

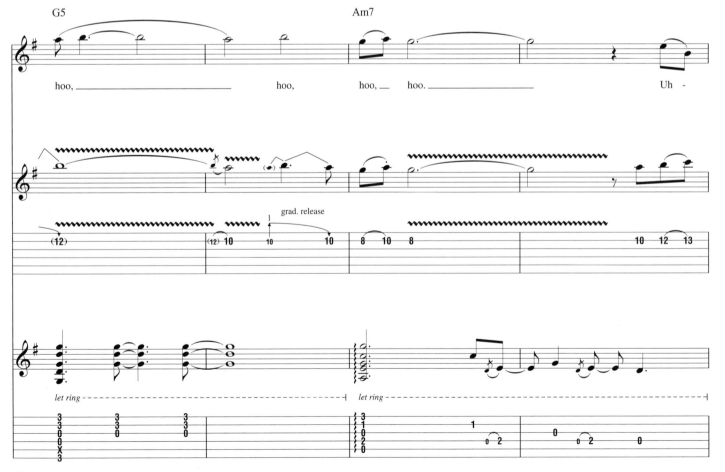

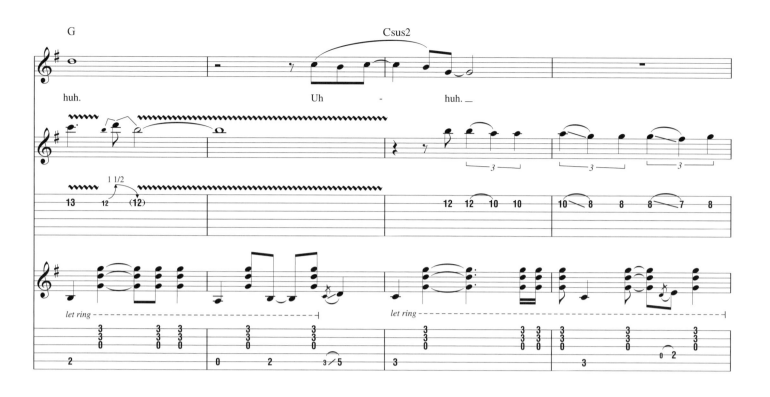

huh.   Uh -   huh.

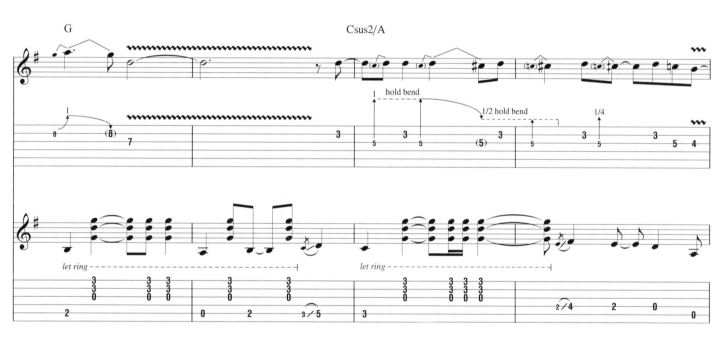

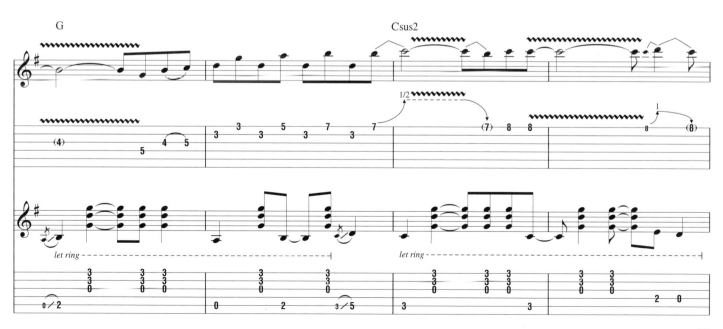

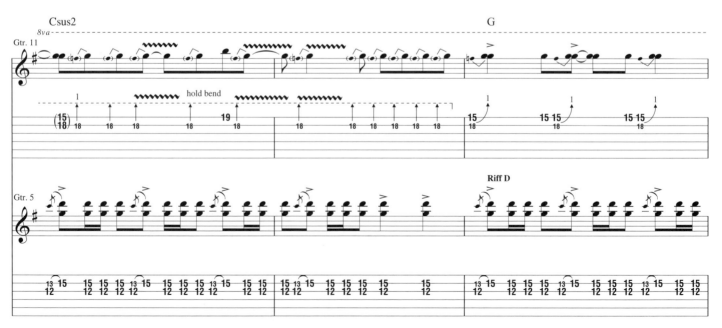

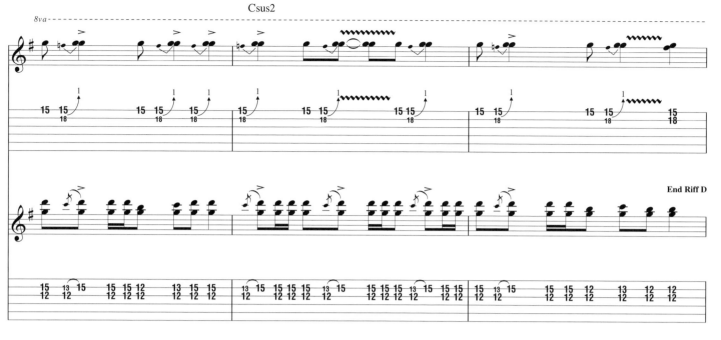

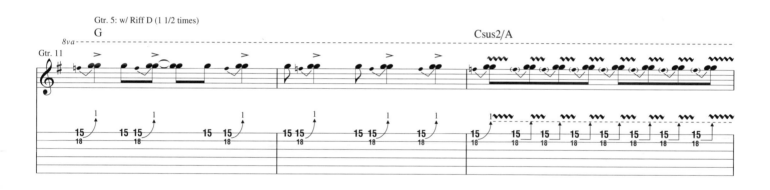

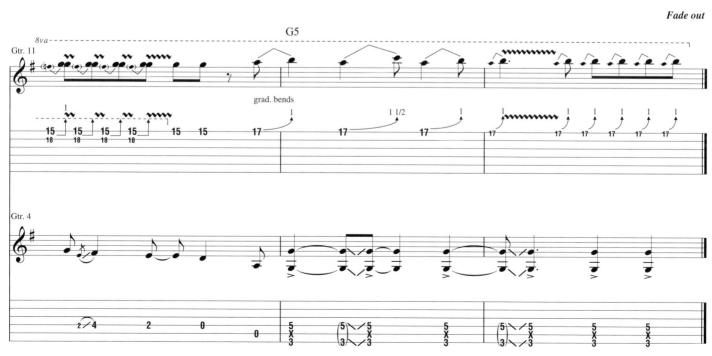

Shine

Words and Music by
Keith Urban and Monty Powell

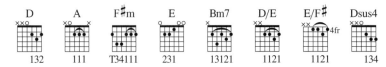

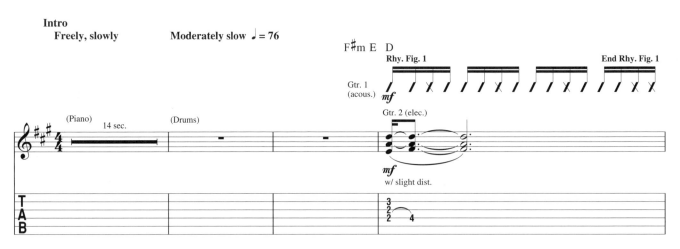

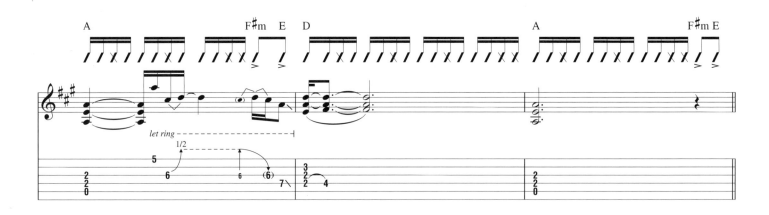

Verse

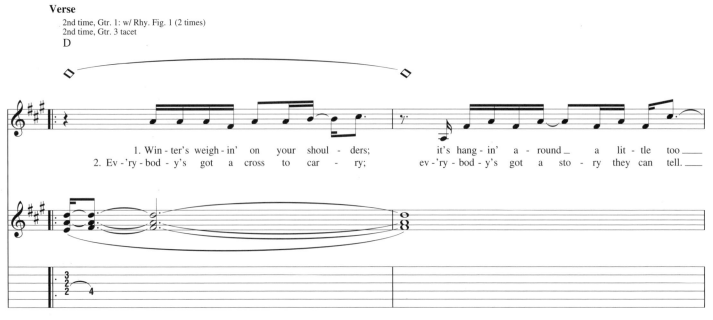

1. Win-ter's weigh-in' on your shoul-ders; it's hang-in' a-round a lit-tle too
2. Ev-'ry-bod-y's got a cross to car-ry; ev-'ry-bod-y's got a sto-ry they can tell.

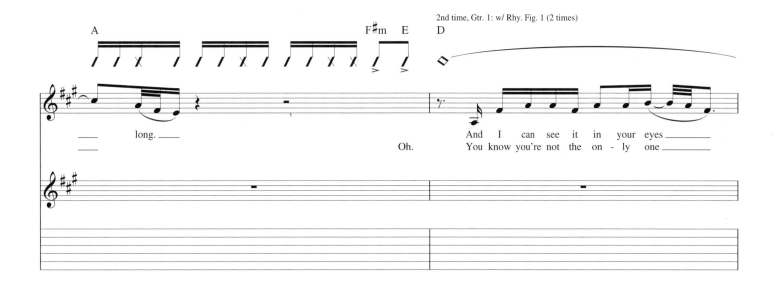

2nd time, Gtr. 1: w/ Rhy. Fig. 1 (2 times)

long.

Oh.

And I can see it in your eyes

You know you're not the on - ly one

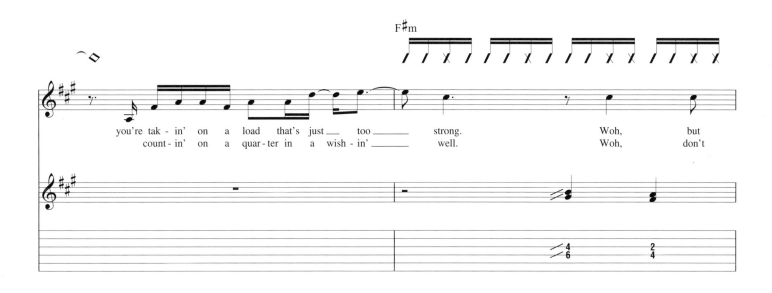

you're tak - in' on a load that's just too strong. Woh, but

count - in' on a quar - ter in a wish - in' well. Woh, don't

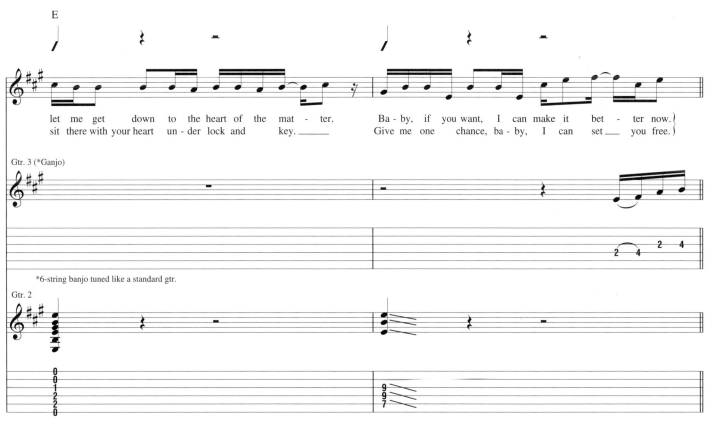

let me get down to the heart of the mat - ter. Ba - by, if you want, I can make it bet - ter now.

sit there with your heart un - der lock and key. Give me one chance, ba - by, I can set you free.

Gtr. 3 (*Ganjo)

*6-string banjo tuned like a standard gtr.

Gtr. 2

21

Chorus

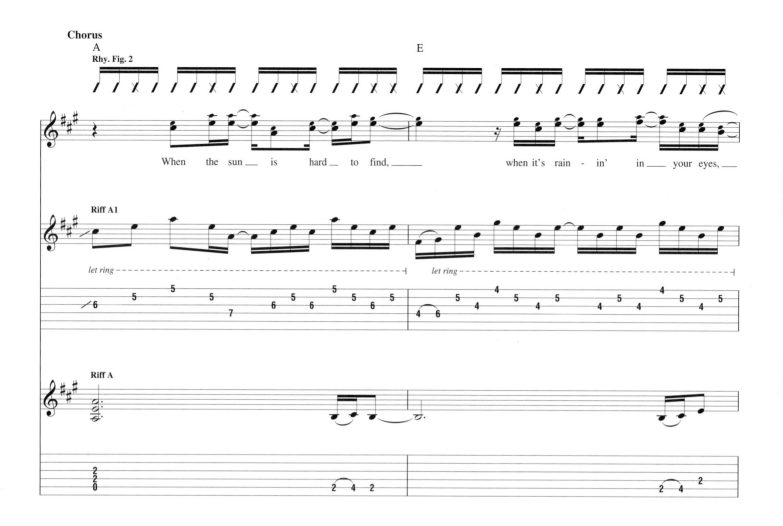

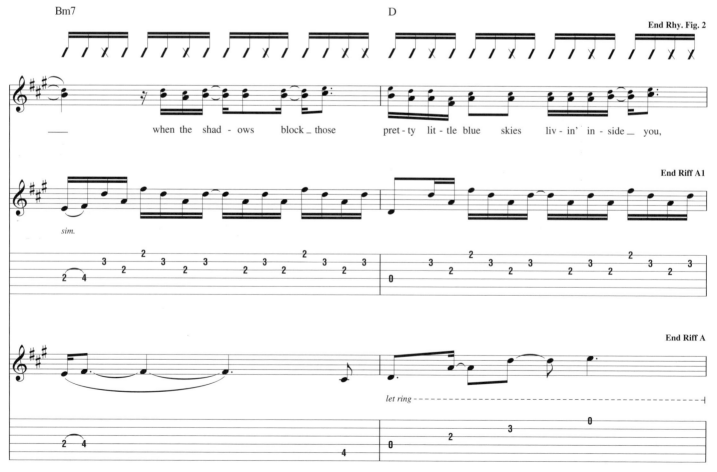

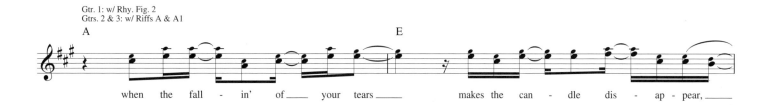

when the fall - in' of ___ your tears ___ makes the can - dle dis - ap - pear, ___

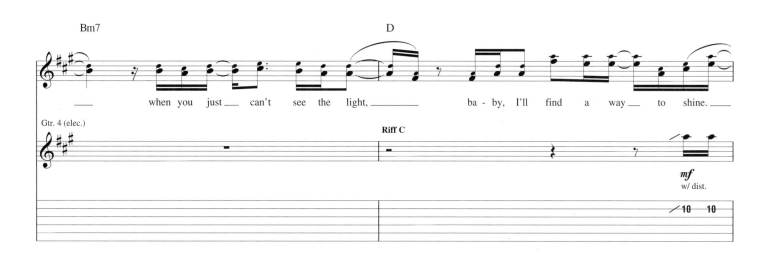

___ when you just ___ can't see the light, _____ ba - by, I'll find a way ___ to shine. ___

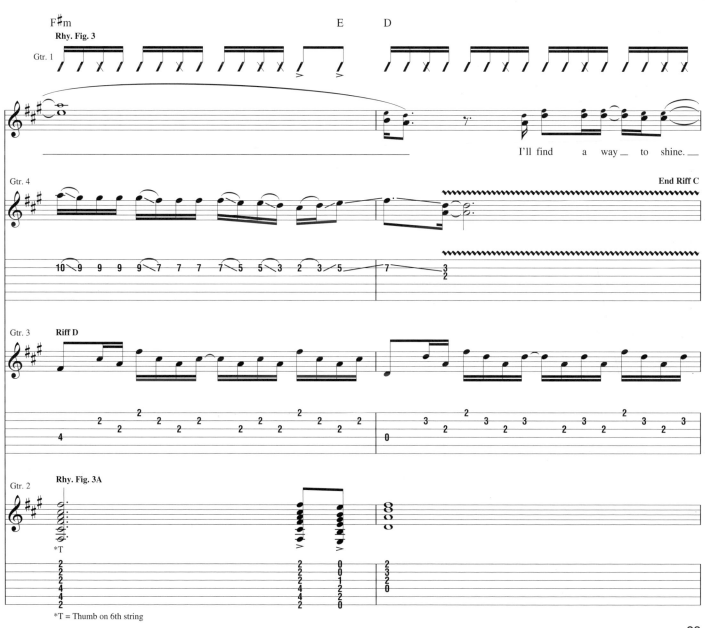

I'll find a way ___ to shine. ___

*T = Thumb on 6th string

24

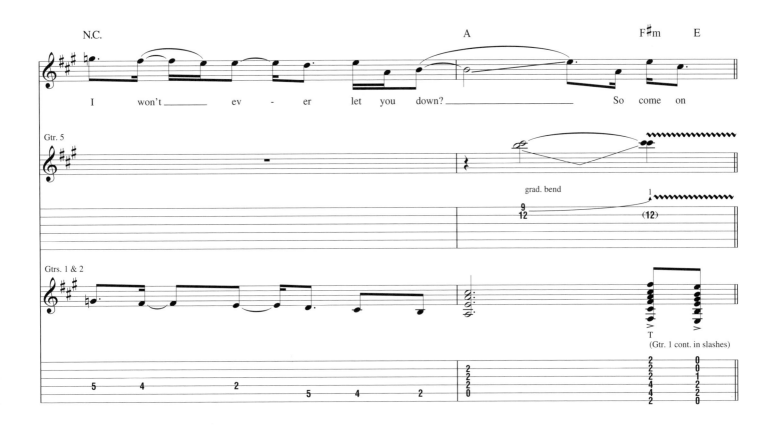

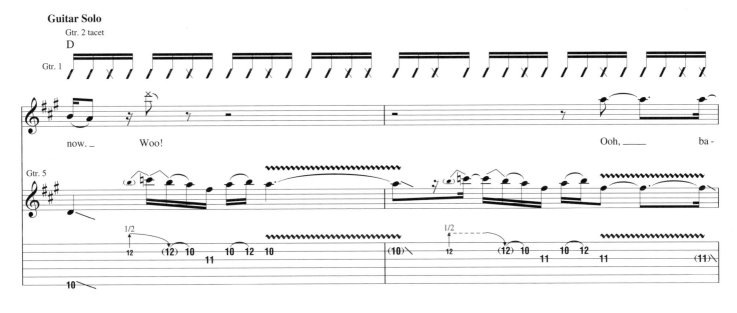

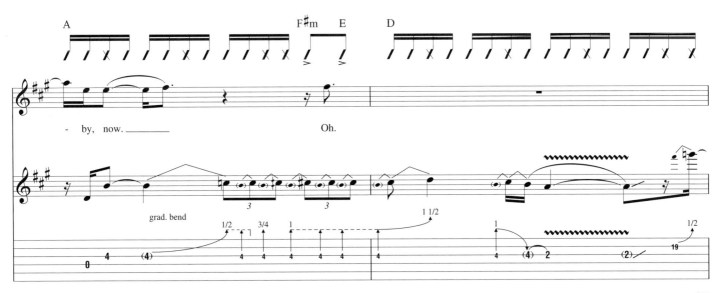

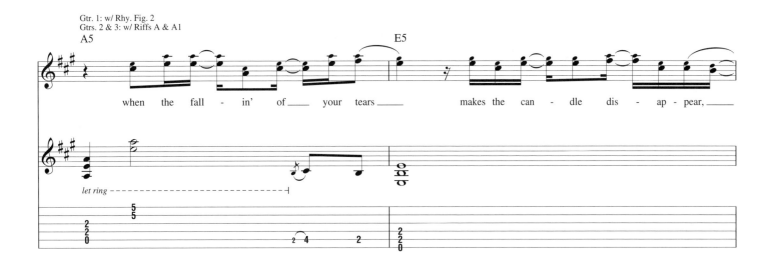

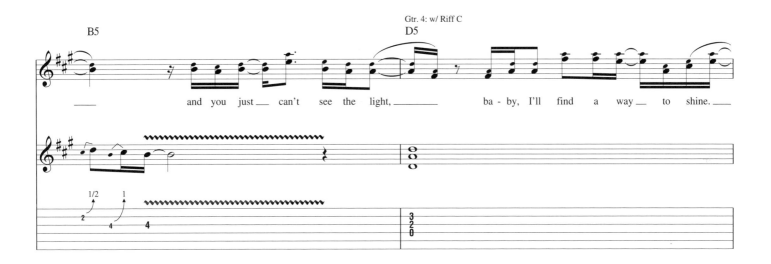

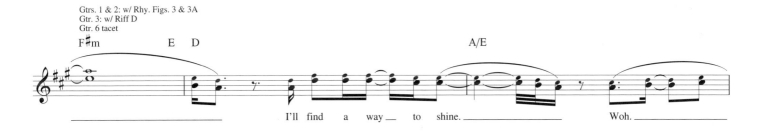

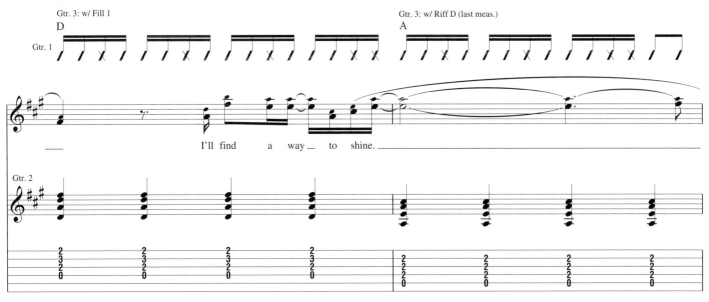

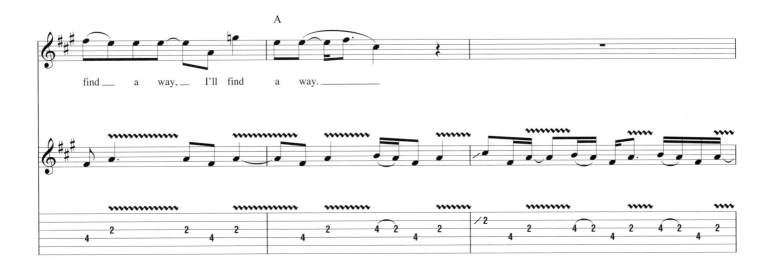

find ___ a way, ___ I'll find ___ a way. ___

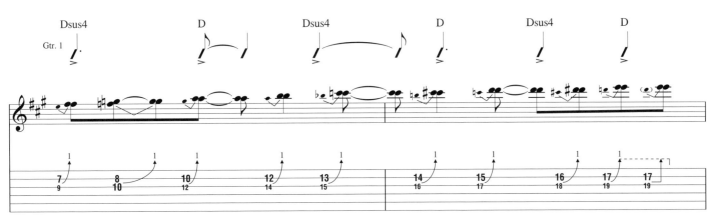

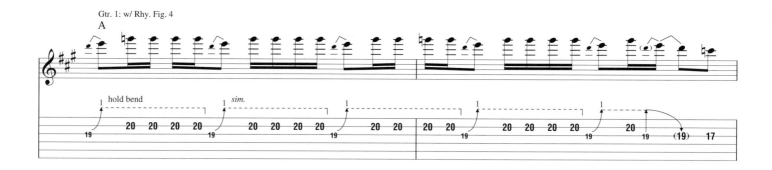

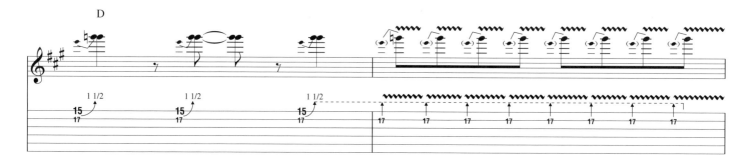

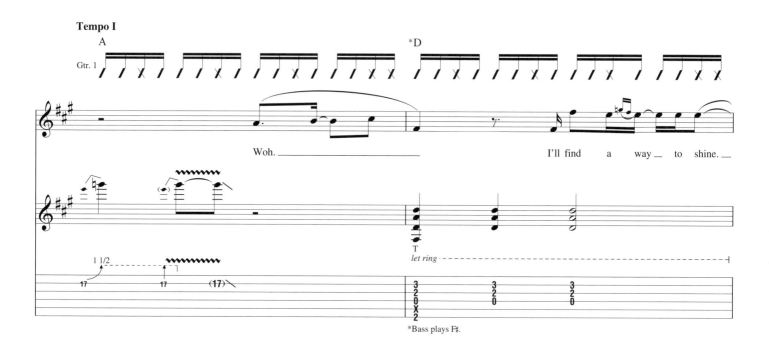

*Bass plays F♯.

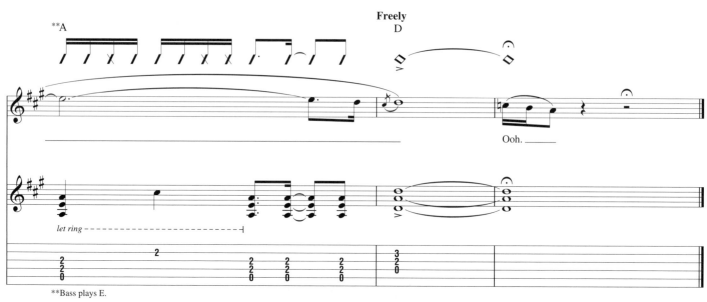

**Bass plays E.

I Told You So

Words and Music by
Keith Urban

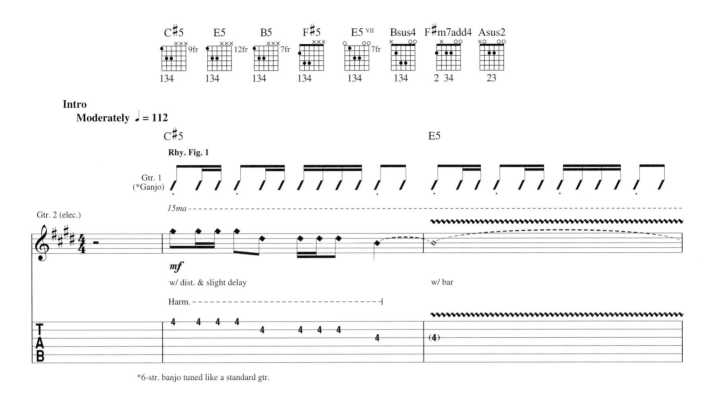

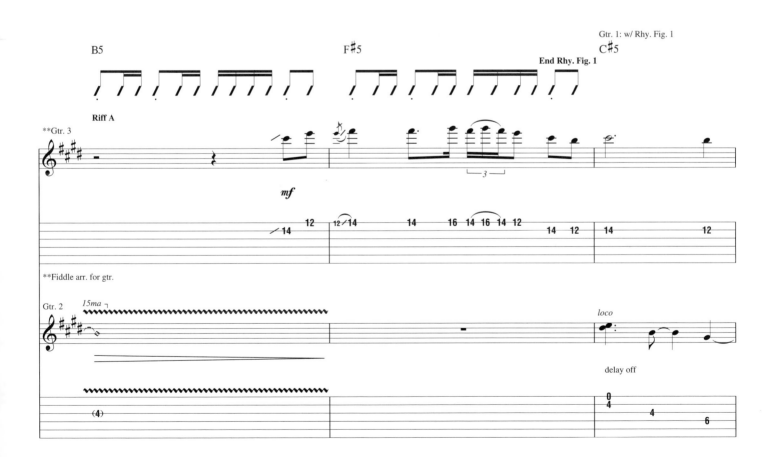

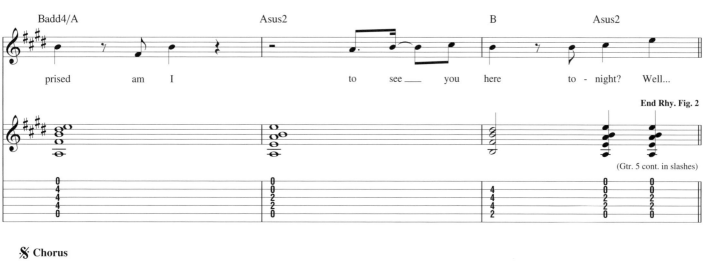

Badd4/A   Asus2   B   Asus2

prised am I   to see ___ you here   to - night? Well...

End Rhy. Fig. 2

(Gtr. 5 cont. in slashes)

§ **Chorus**

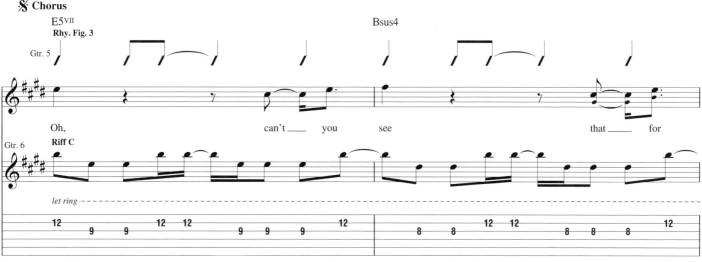

E5ᵛᴵᴵ   Bsus4

Rhy. Fig. 3

Gtr. 5

Oh,   can't ___ you see   that ___ for

Gtr. 6 **Riff C**

let ring -

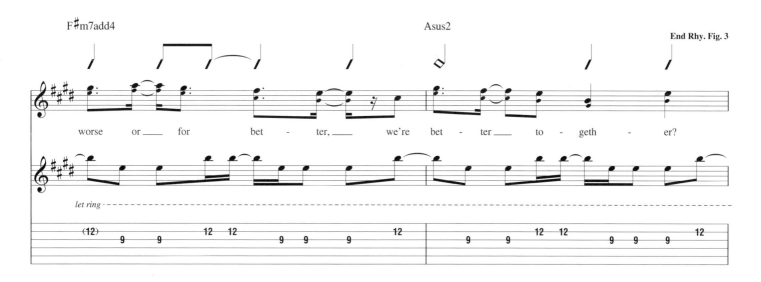

F#m7add4   Asus2

End Rhy. Fig. 3

worse or ___ for bet - ter, ___ we're bet - ter ___ to - geth - er?

let ring -

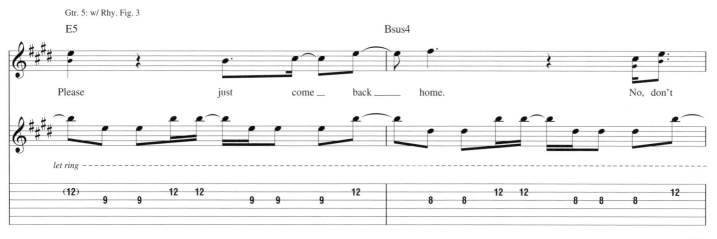

Gtr. 5: w/ Rhy. Fig. 3

E5   Bsus4

Please   just come ___ back ___ home.   No, don't

let ring -

Outro

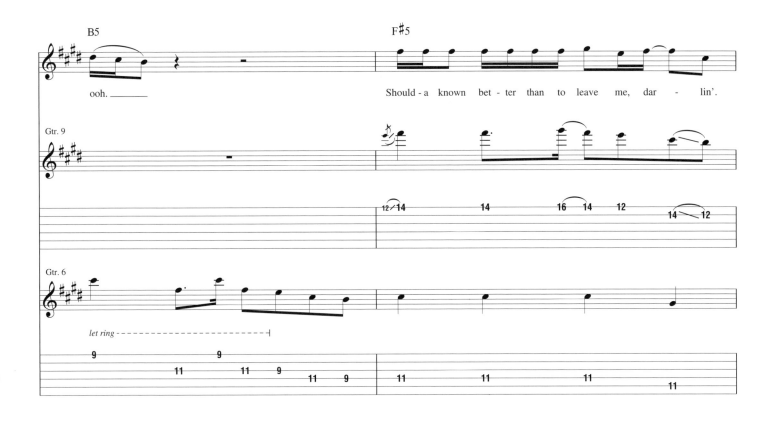

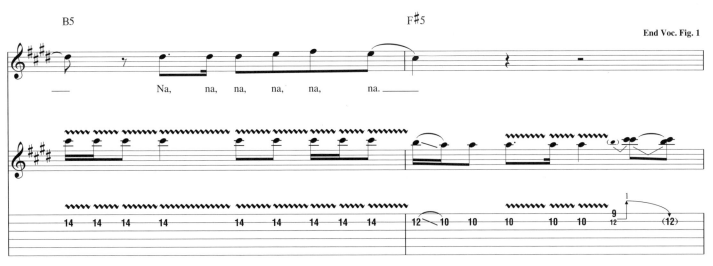

I Can't Stop Loving You

Words and Music by
Billy Nicholls

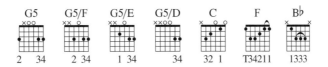

Tune down 1/2 step:
(low to high) E♭-A♭-D♭-G♭-B♭-E♭

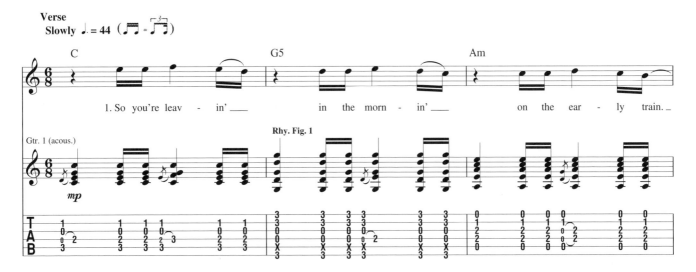

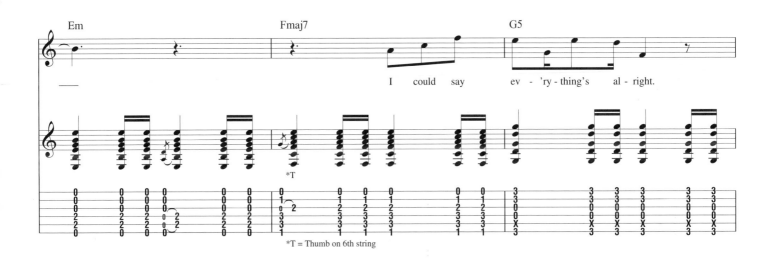

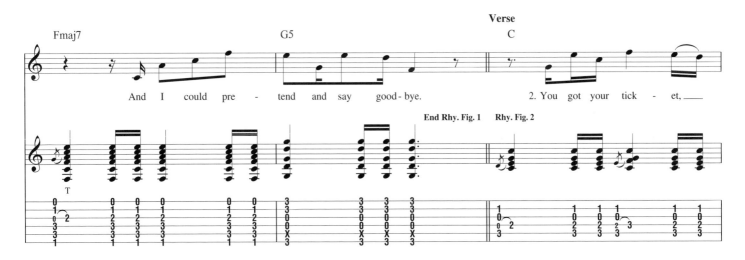

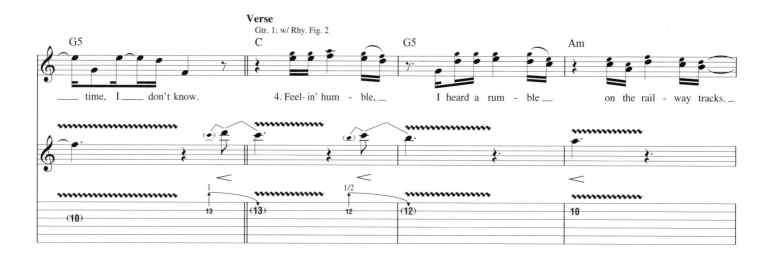

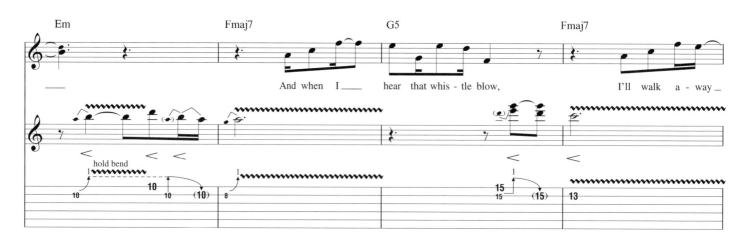

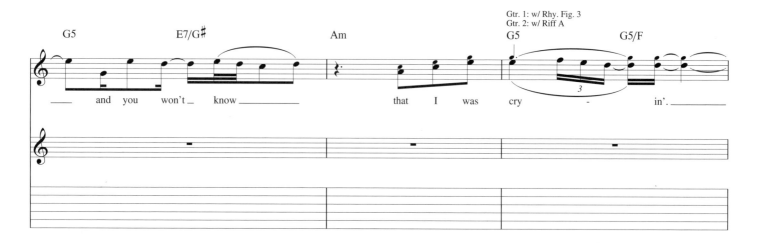

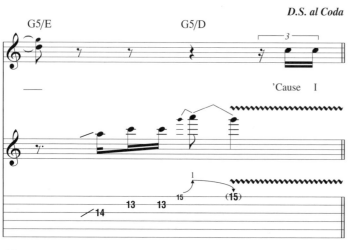

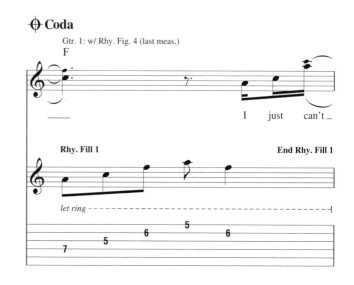

Won't Let You Down

Words and Music by
Keith Urban

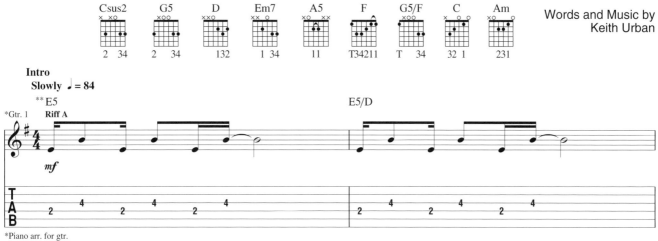

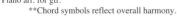

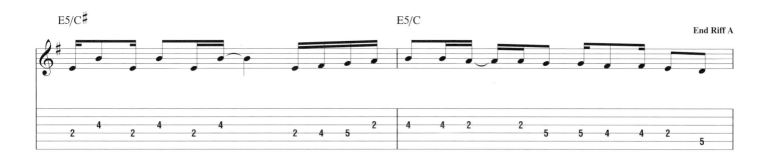

*Piano arr. for gtr.
**Chord symbols reflect overall harmony.

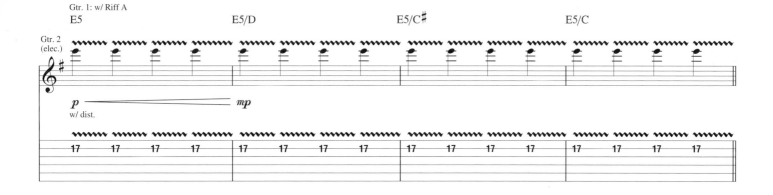

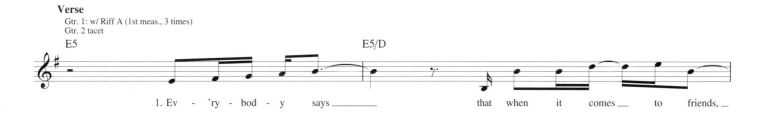

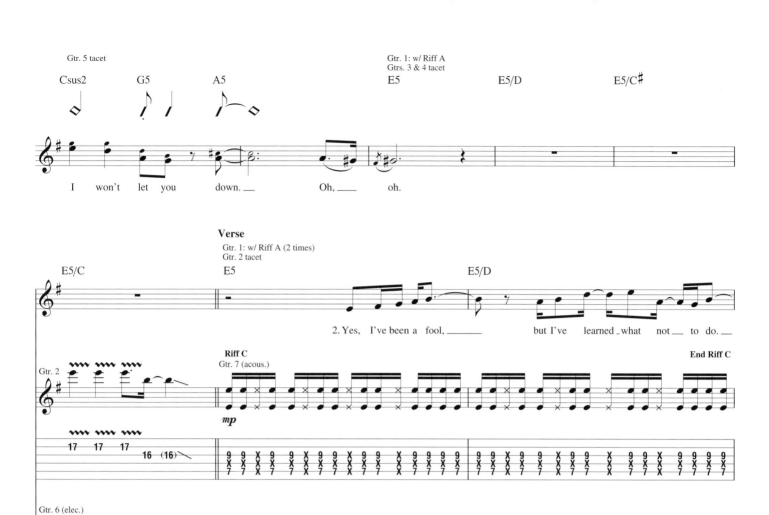

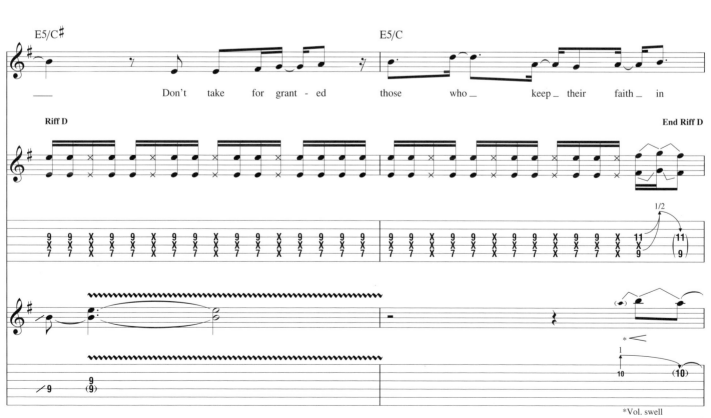

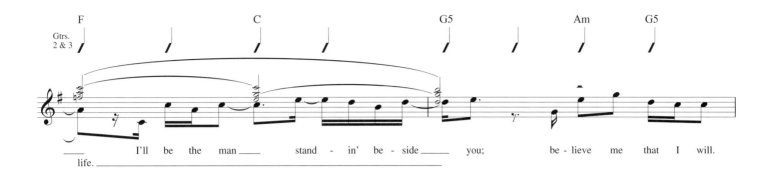

I'll be the man ___ stand - in' be - side ___ you; be - lieve me that I will.
life. ___

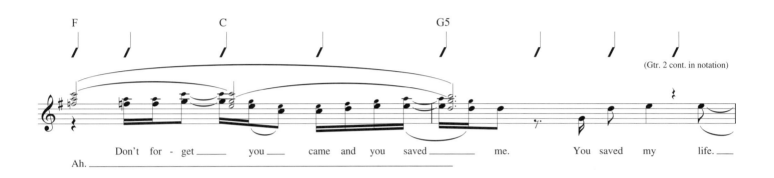

Don't for - get ___ you ___ came and you saved ___ me. You saved my life. ___
Ah. ___

(Gtr. 2 cont. in notation)

Ah.) ___

Chorus

Gtrs. 2 & 3 tacet

Yeah, I'll catch ___ you when ___ you fall ___ 'cause I'm the one ___ who loves ___ you.

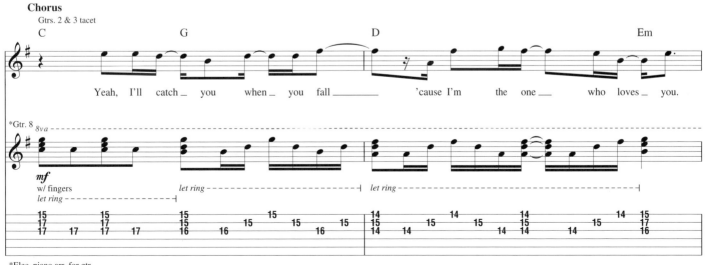

*Gtr. 8 8va

mf
w/ fingers
let ring
let ring
let ring

*Elec. piano arr. for gtr.

53

Faster Car

Words and Music by
Keith Urban

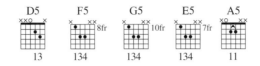

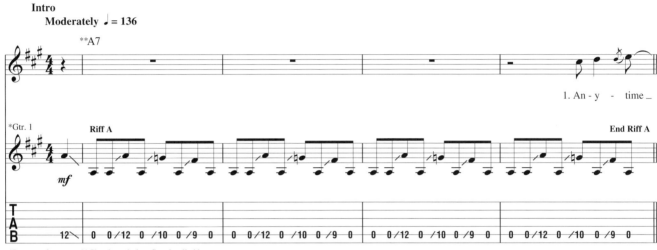

*Bass arr. for gtr.   **Chord symbols reflect implied harmony.

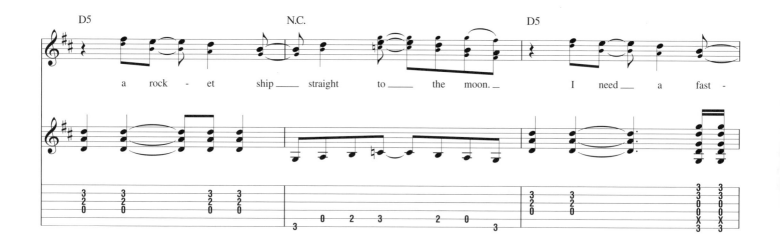

a rock-et ship____ straight to____ the moon.____ I need____ a fast-

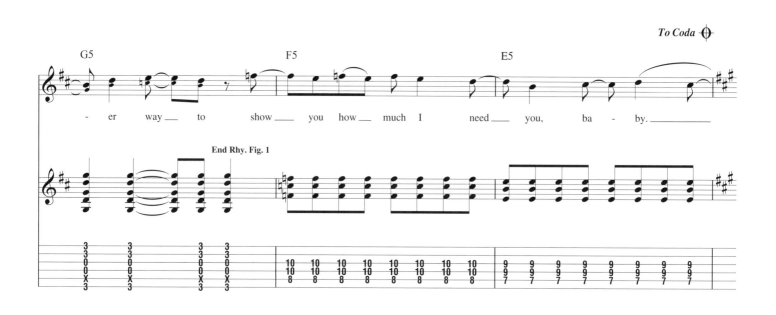

To Coda ⊕

-er way____ to show____ you how____ much I need____ you, ba-by.____

End Rhy. Fig. 1

Gtr. 2 tacet

A7

____ Oh.

Gtr. 4 (*Ganjo)

mf

*6-string banjo tuned like a standard gtr.

Gtr. 3

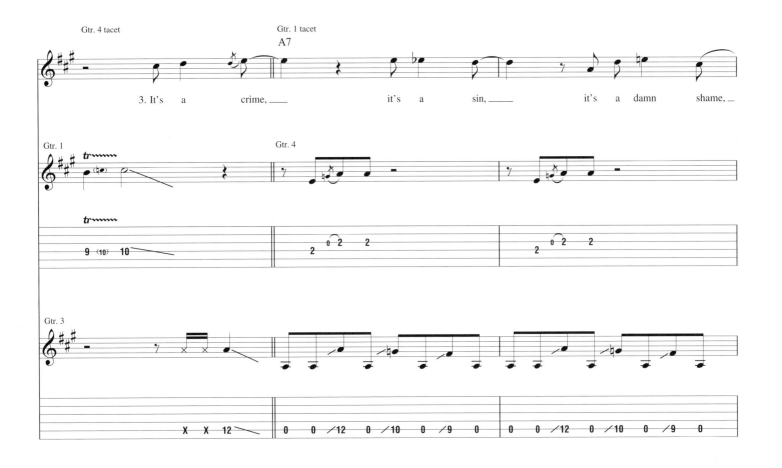

3. It's a crime, ___ it's a sin, ___ it's a damn shame, ___

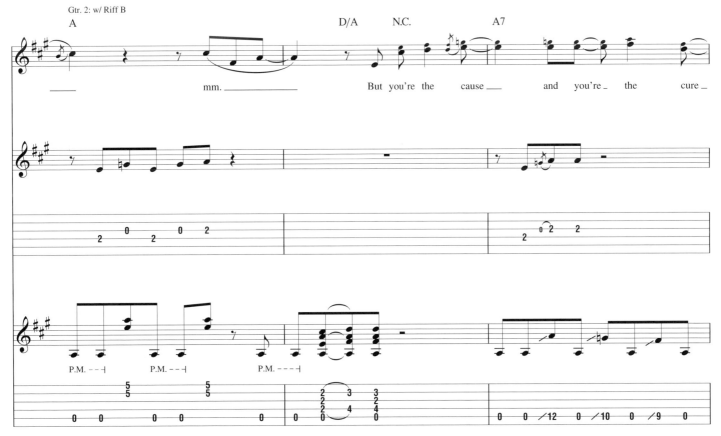

mm. _____ But you're the cause ___ and you're ___ the cure ___

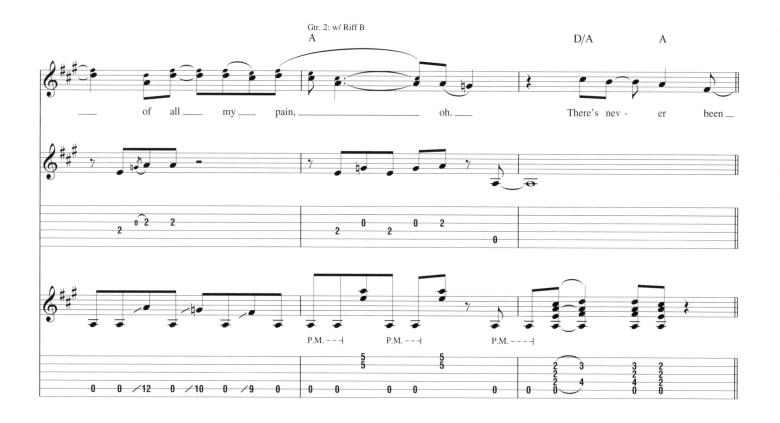

Pre-Chorus

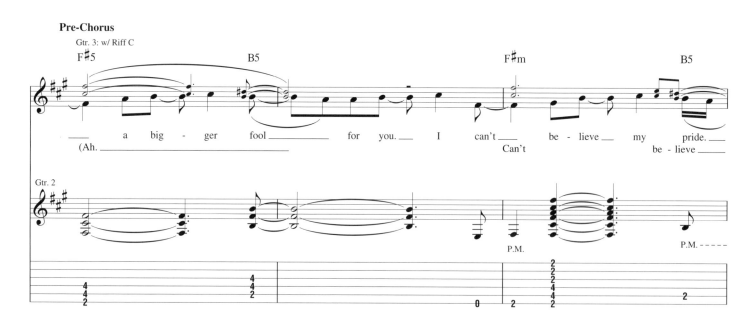

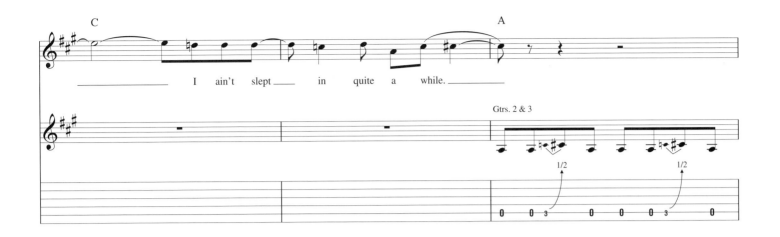

I ain't slept ____ in quite a while. ____

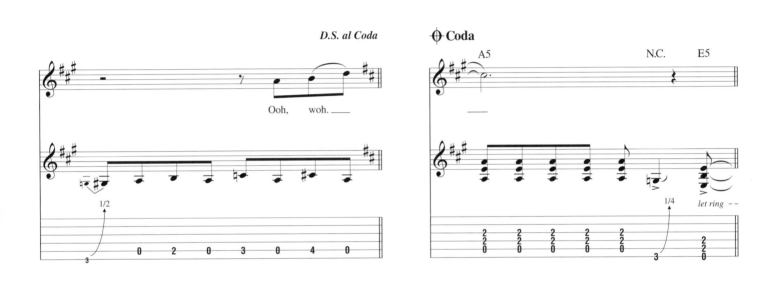

D.S. al Coda

Coda

Ooh, woh. ____

Interlude

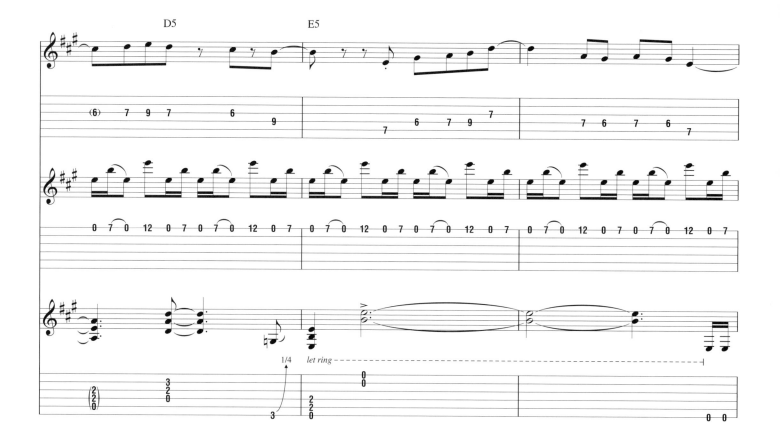

Ooh, _____ ooh, _____

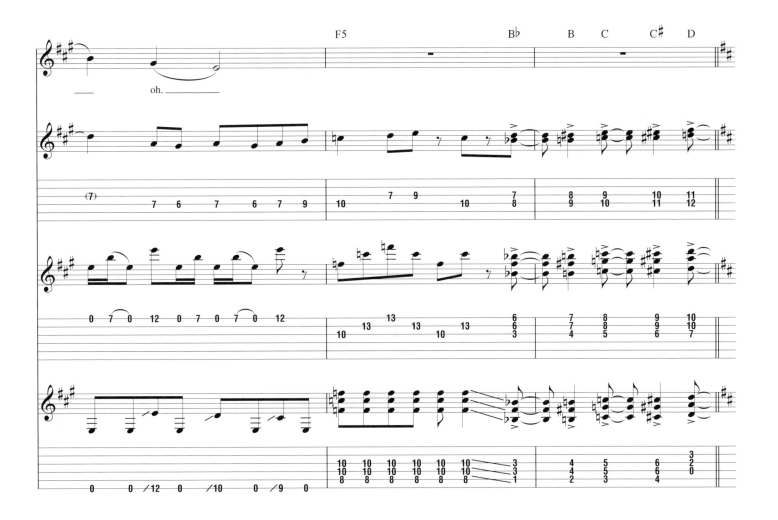

Chorus

Gtrs. 4 & 5 tacet

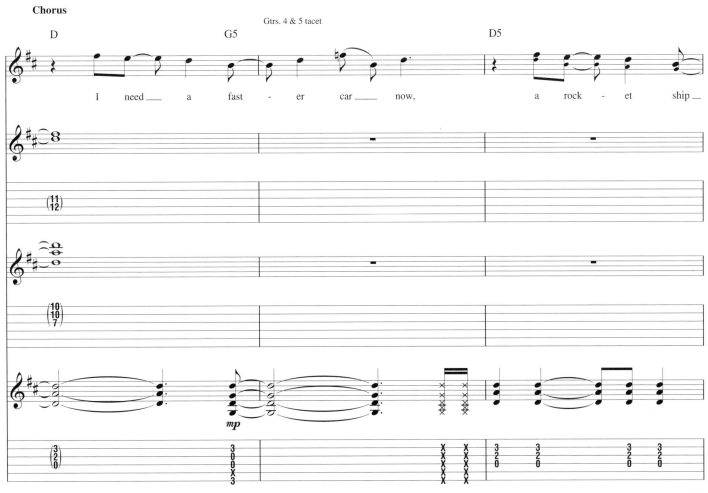

I need ___ a fast - er car ___ now,   a rock - et ship ___

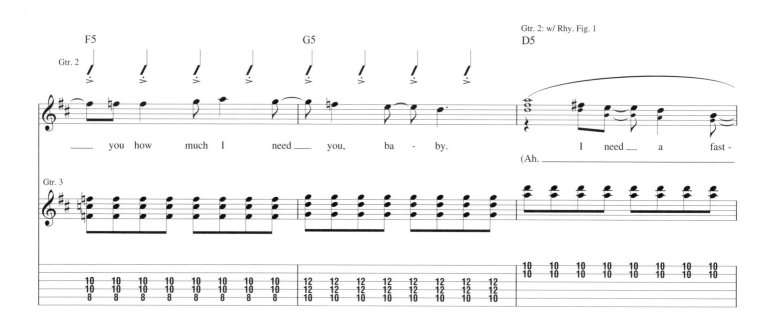
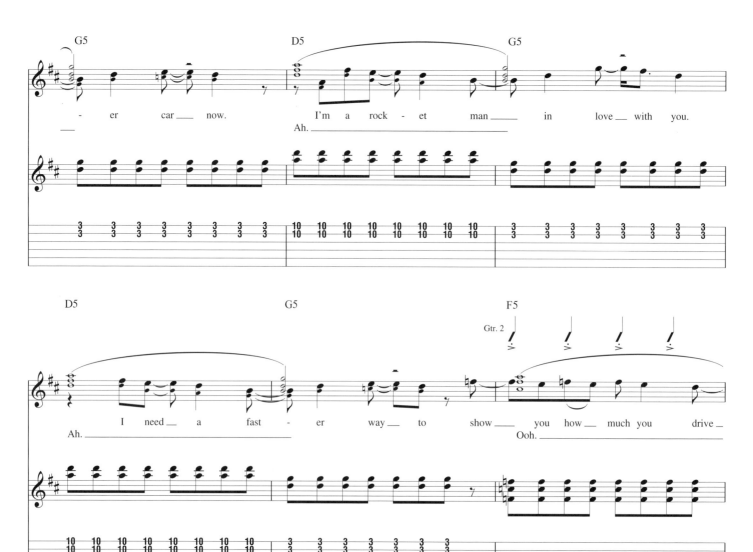

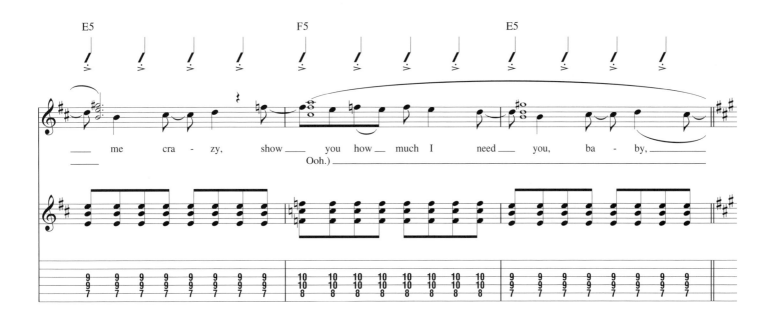

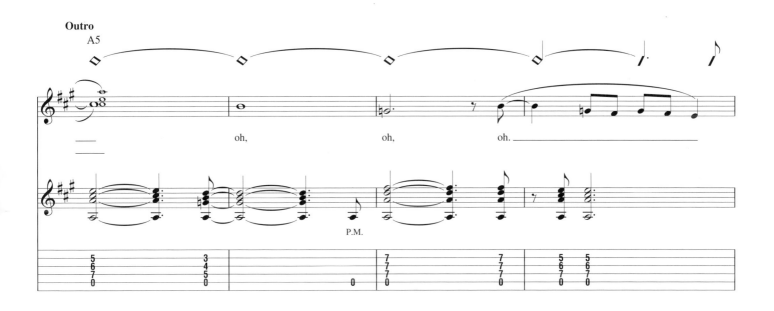

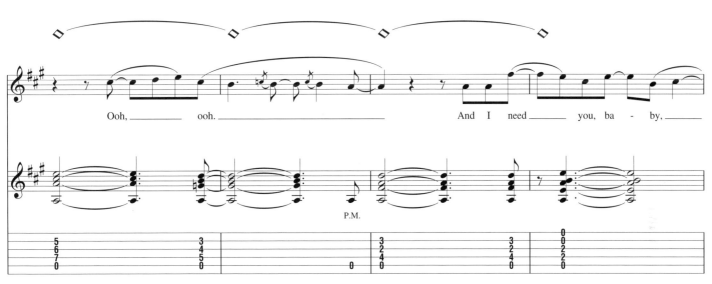

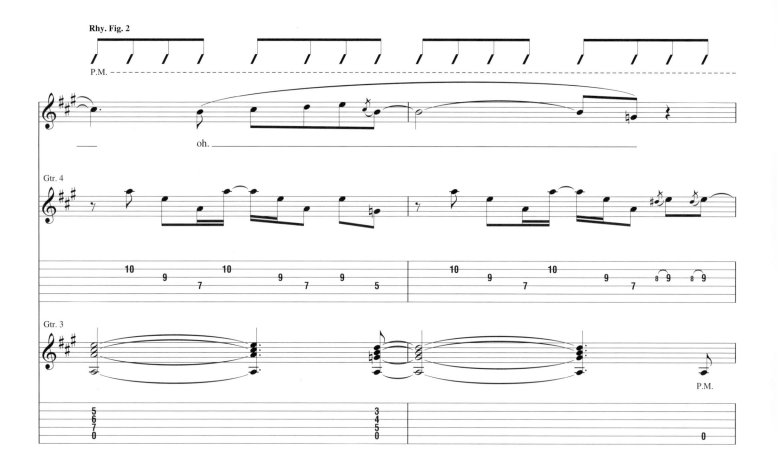

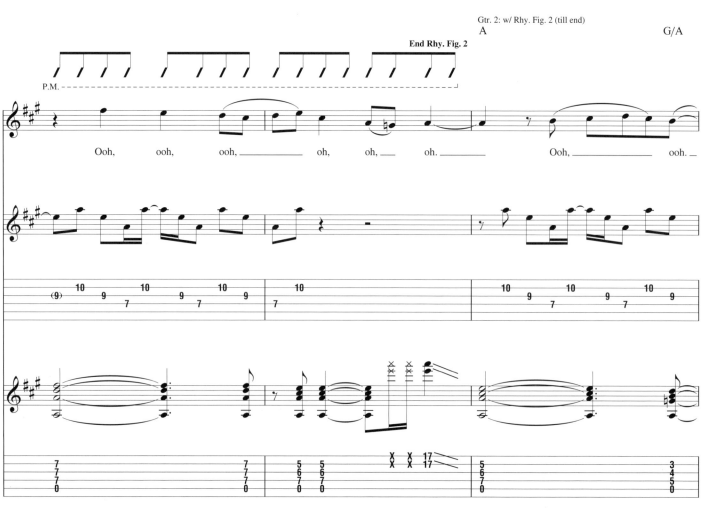

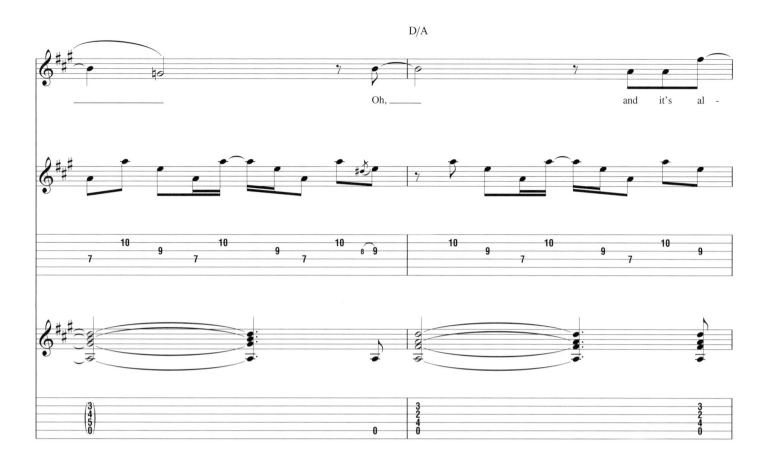

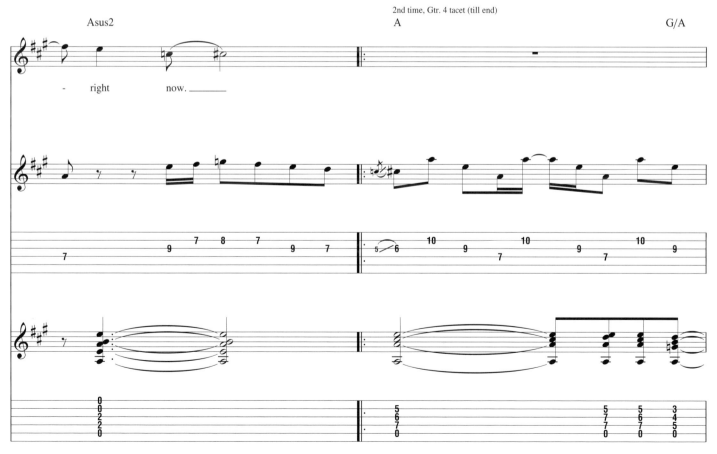

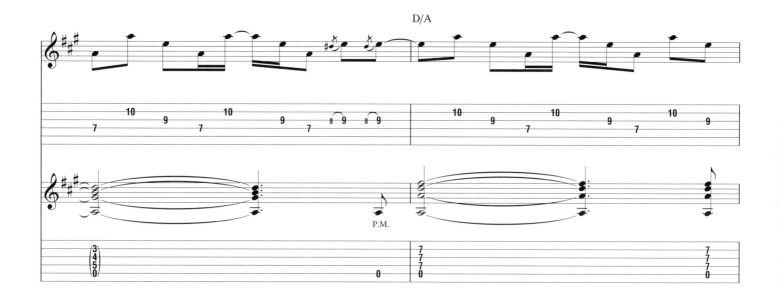

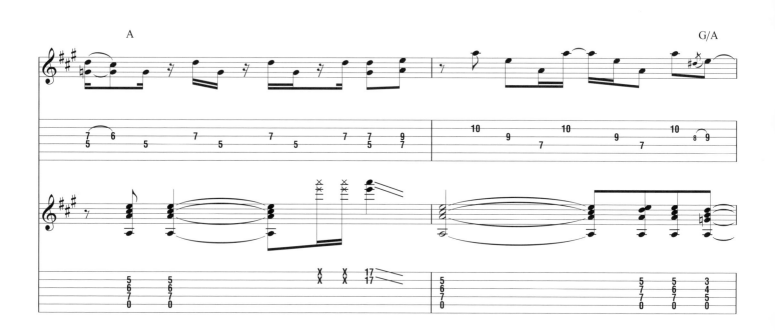

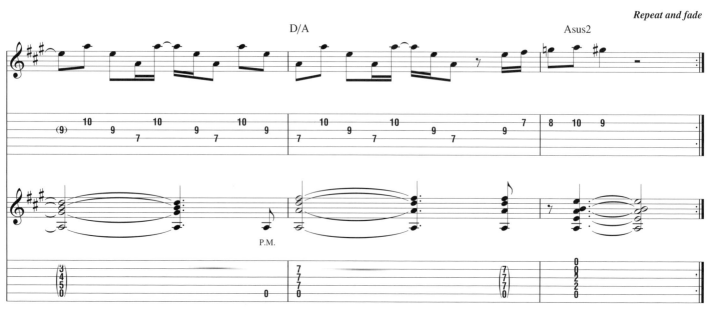

Stupid Boy

Words and Music by
Sarah Buxton, Dave Berg
and Deanna Bryant

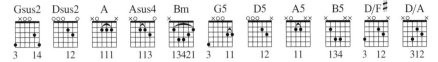

Drop D tuning, capo I:
(low to high) D-A-D-G-B-E

Intro

Slowly ♩ = 76

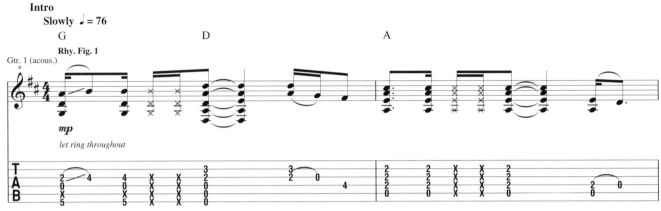

*All music sounds a half step higher than written due to capo.

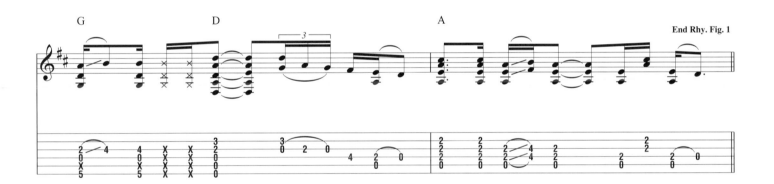

Verse

1. Well, she was pre - cious like a flow - er. She grew wild, ___

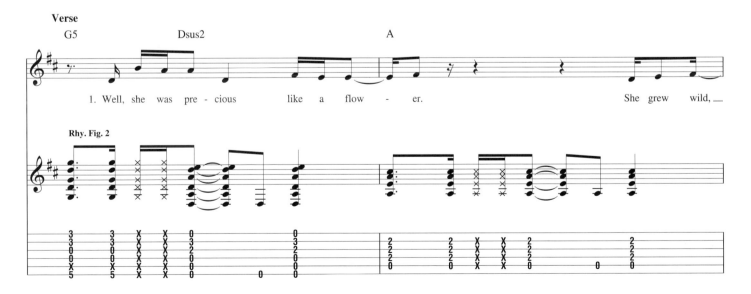

e - ven knew___ she had___ a choice,___ and that's what hap - pens when ___ the on - ly voice___

___ she hears___ is tell - ing her ___ she ___ can't. ___ Stu - pid boy, ___

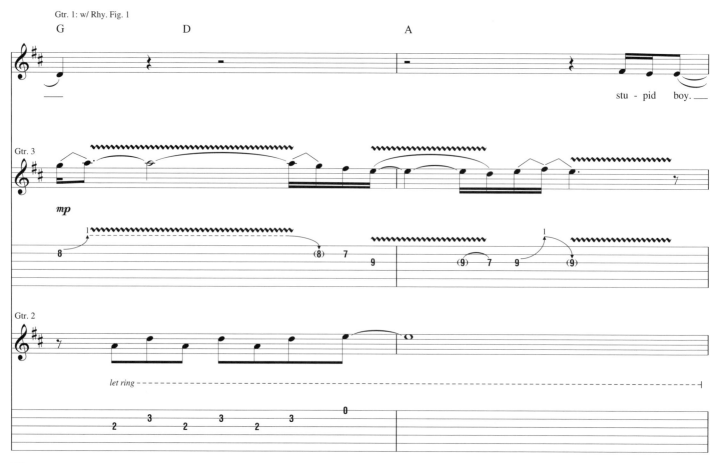

stu - pid boy. ___

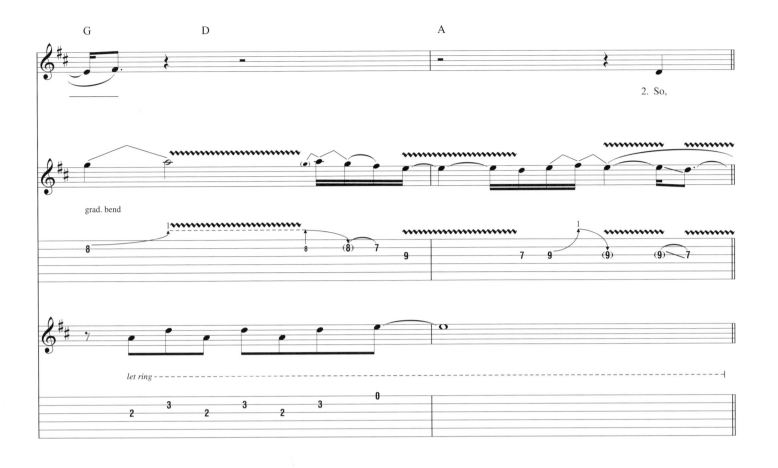

2. So,

Verse

Gtr. 1: w/ Rhy. Fig. 2

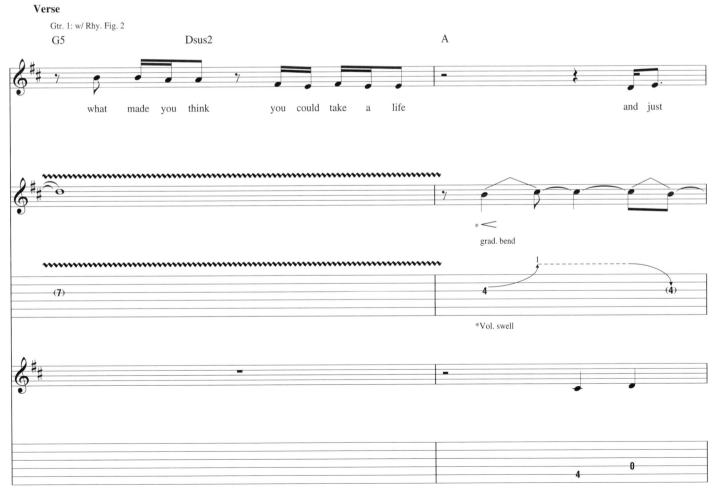

what made you think you could take a life and just

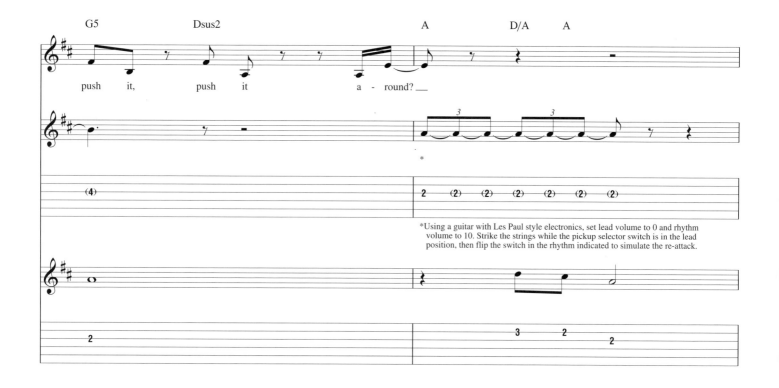

*Using a guitar with Les Paul style electronics, set lead volume to 0 and rhythm volume to 10. Strike the strings while the pickup selector switch is in the lead position, then flip the switch in the rhythm indicated to simulate the re-attack.

push it,   push   it   a - round? __

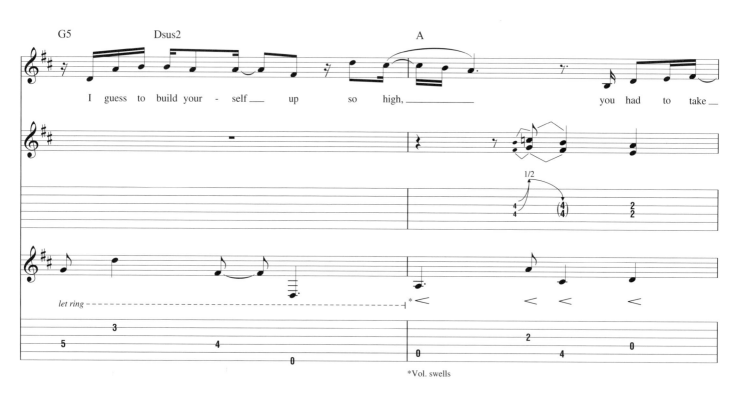

I   guess   to   build   your - self __   up   so   high, _____   you   had   to   take __

*Vol. swells

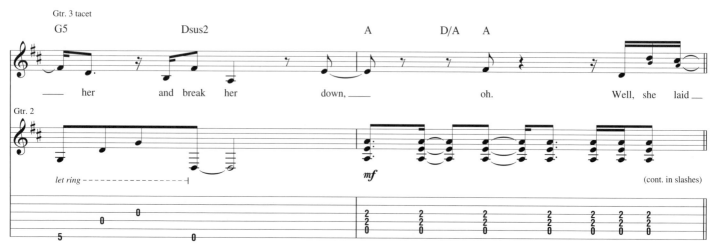

Gtr. 3 tacet

Gtr. 2

__ her   and   break   her   down, __   oh.   Well,   she   laid __

(cont. in slashes)

Chorus

her heart and soul right in your hands, and you stole

her ev-'ry dream and you crushed her plans. She nev-er

e-ven knew she had a choice and that's what hap-pens when the on-ly voice

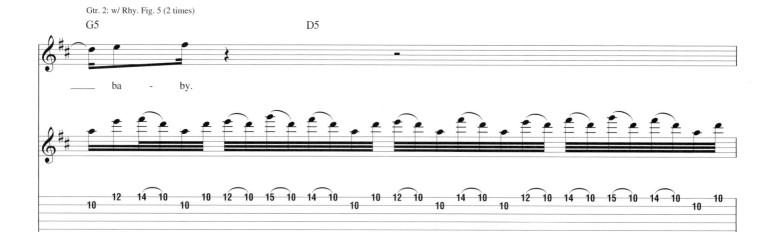

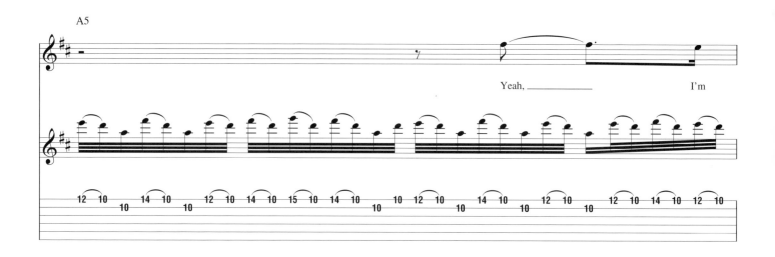

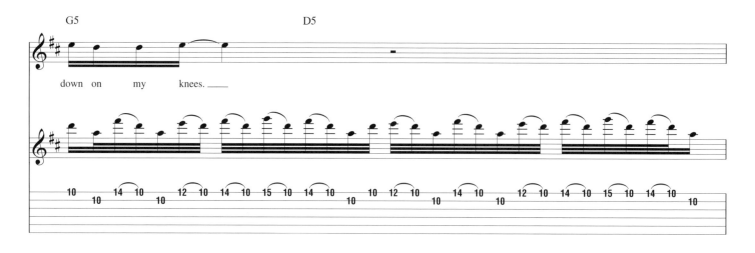

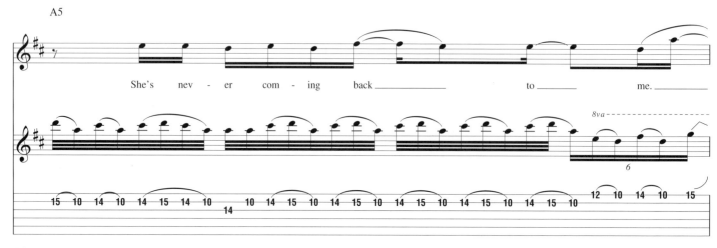

Used To The Pain

Words and Music by
Keith Urban and Darrell Brown

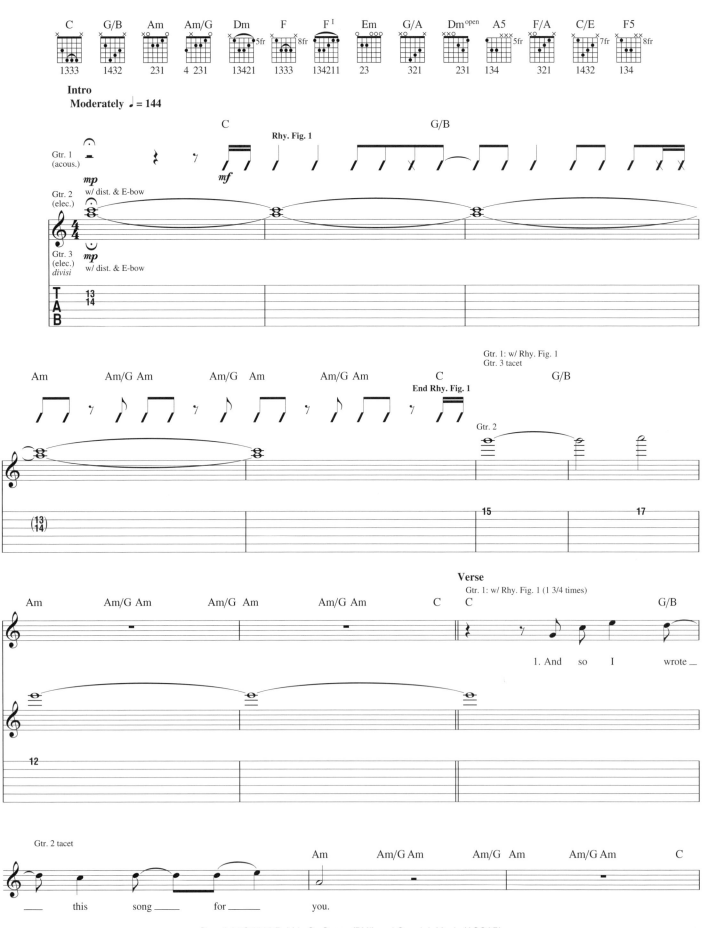

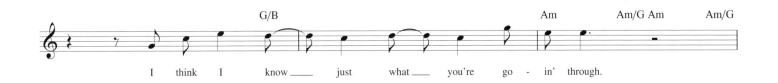

I think I know ____ just what ____ you're go - in' through.

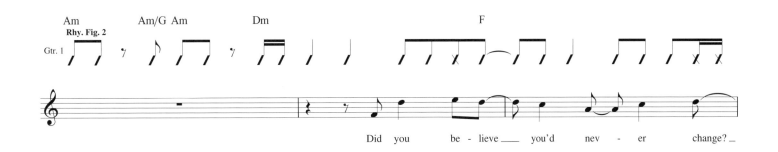

Did you be - lieve ____ you'd nev - er change? ____

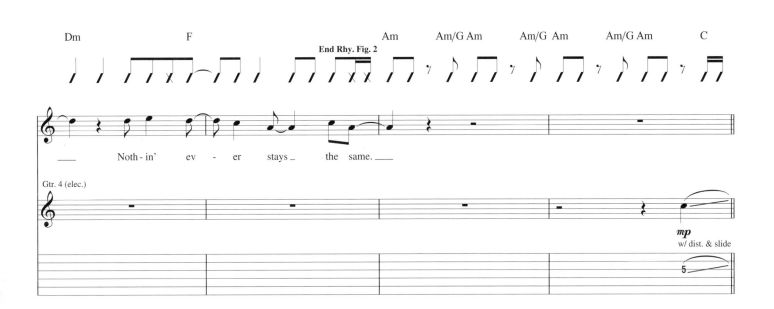

____ Noth - in' ev - er stays ____ the same. ____

Verse

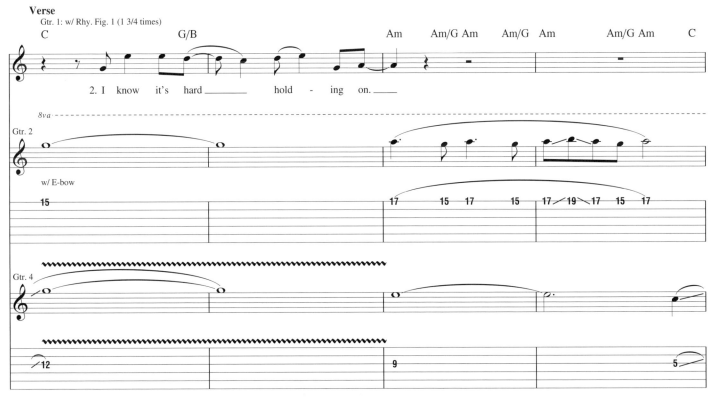

2. I know it's hard _____ hold - ing on. ____

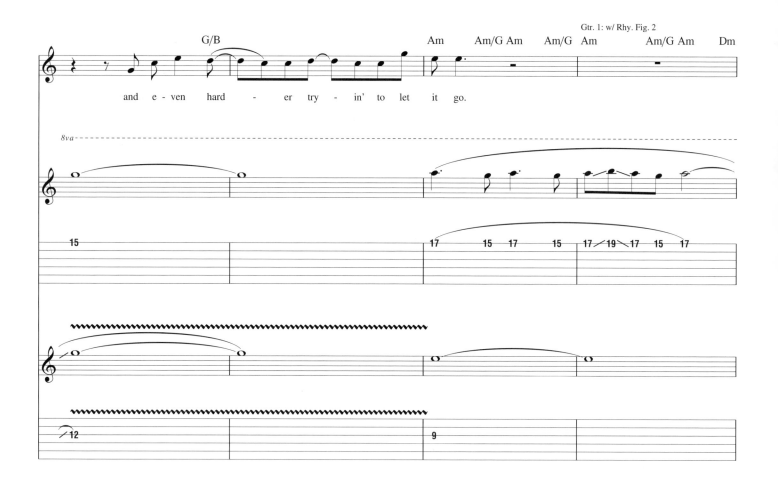

and e-ven hard - er try - in' to let it go.

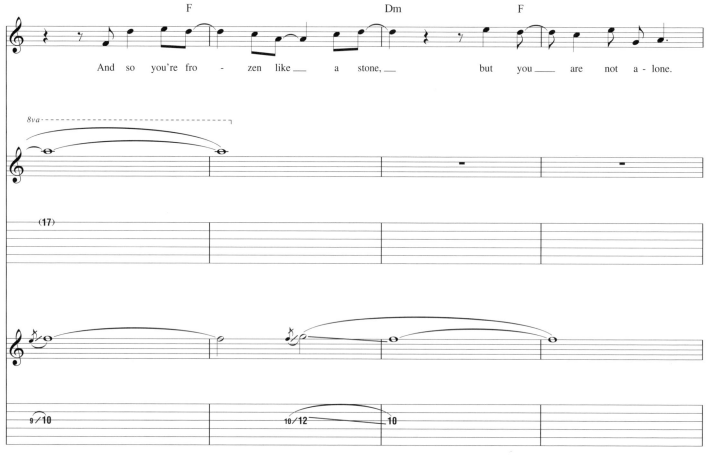

And so you're fro - zen like __ a stone, __ but you __ are not a - lone.

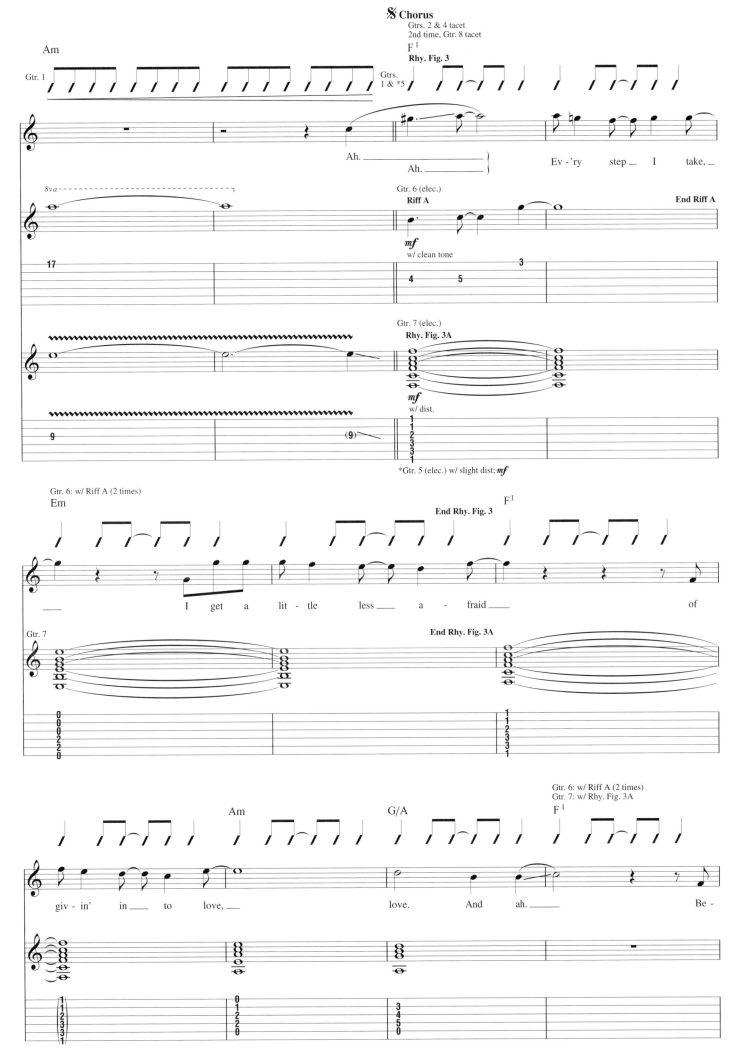

lieve me when ___ I say _____ it gets bet - ter ev - 'ry day, __

To Coda ⊕

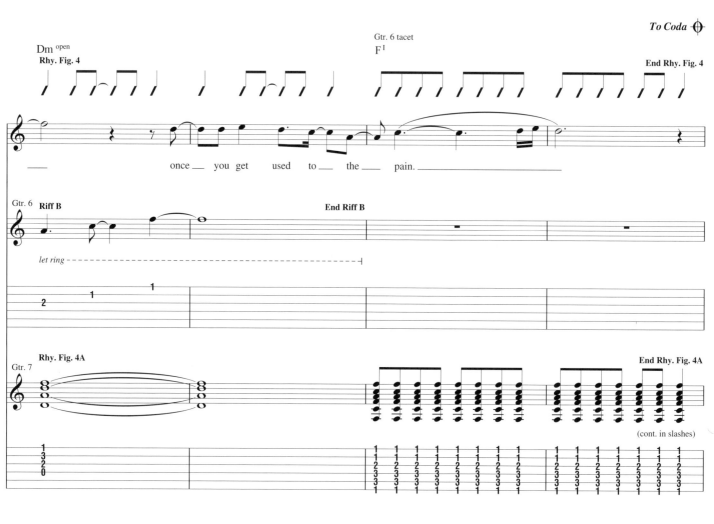

__ once __ you get used to __ the __ pain. _____

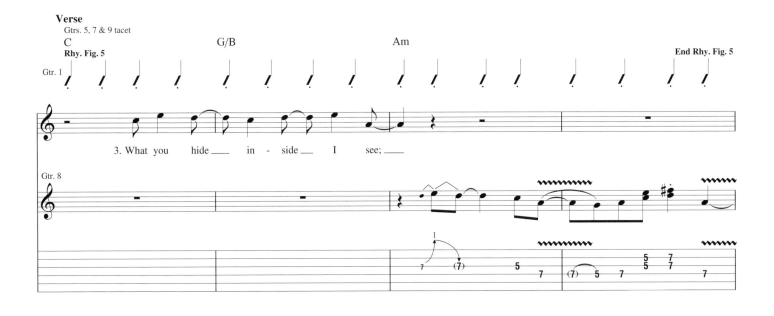

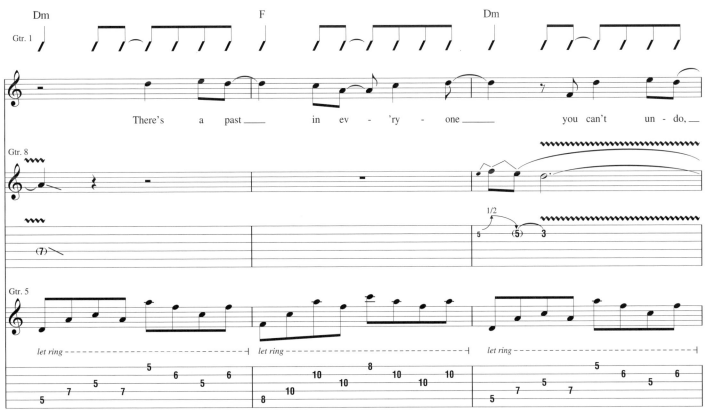

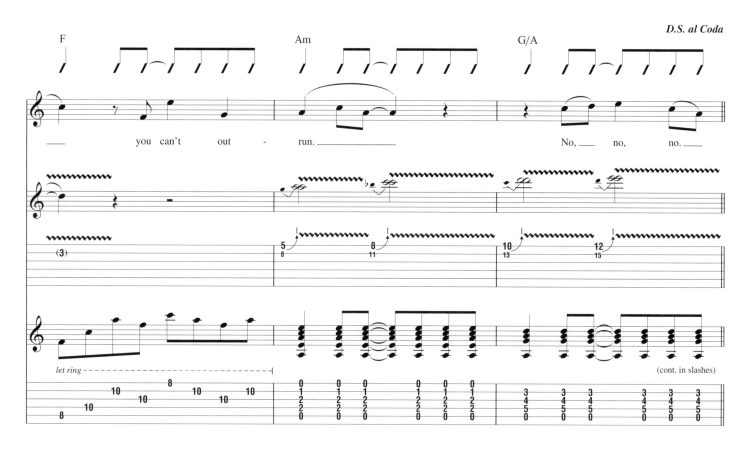

you can't out - run. No, ___ no, no. ___

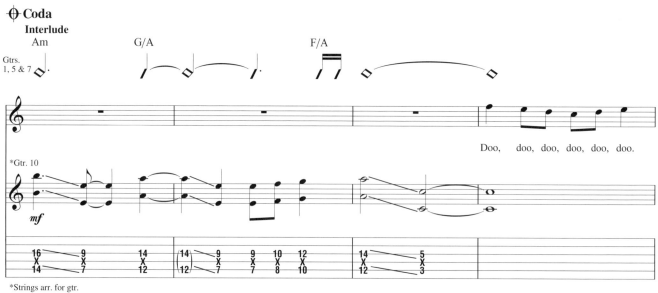

Doo, doo, doo, doo, doo, doo.

*Strings arr. for gtr.

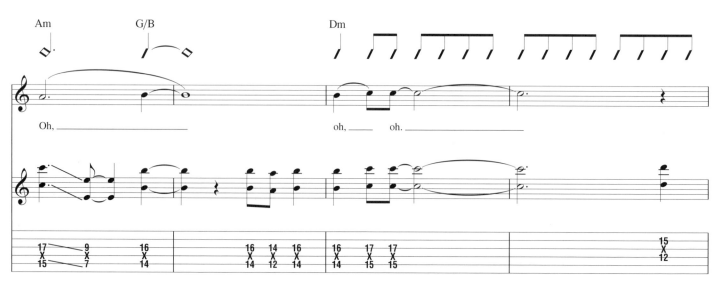

Oh, ___ oh, ___ oh. ___

Raise The Barn

Words and Music by
Keith Urban and Monty Powell

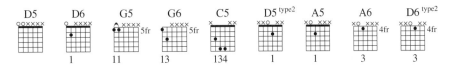

Drop D tuning:
(low to high) D-A-D-G-B-E

Intro
Moderately ♩ = 112

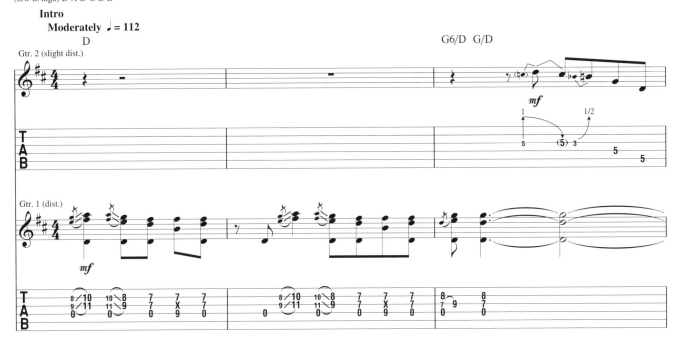

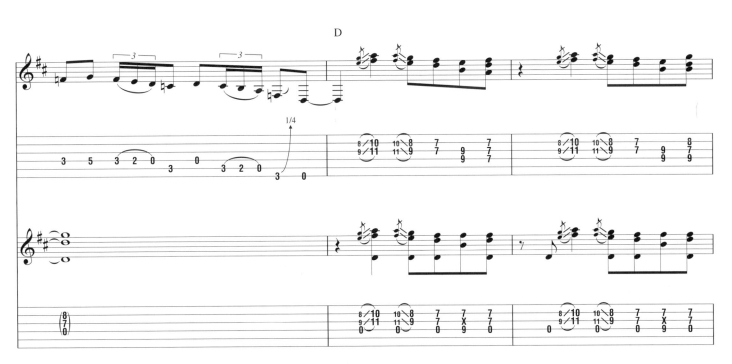

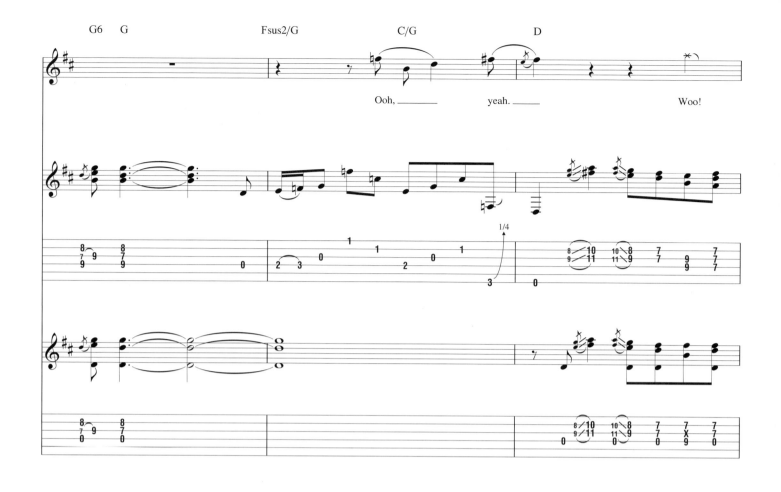

Ooh, _____ yeah. _____ Woo!

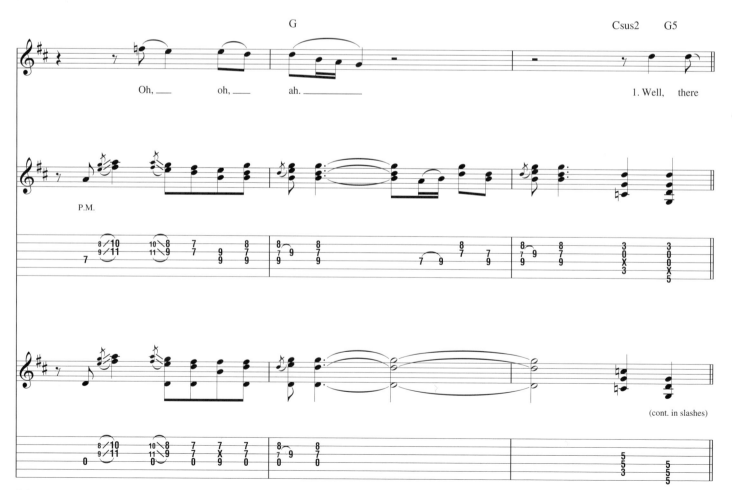

Oh, ___ oh, ___ ah. _____ 1. Well, there

(cont. in slashes)

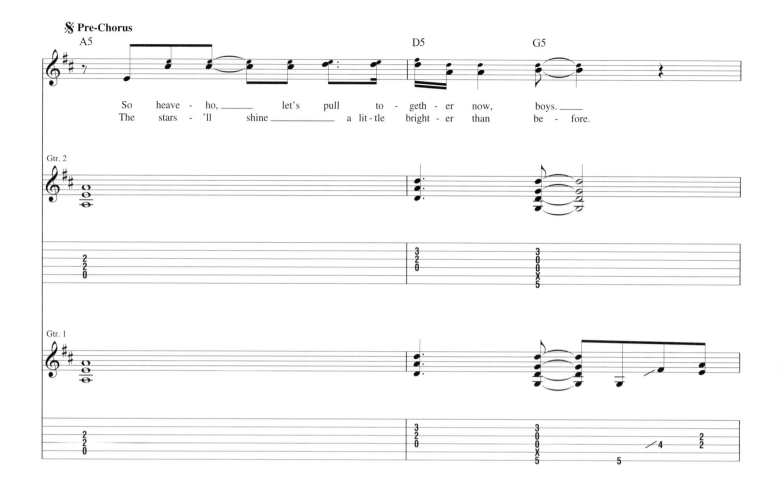

So heave - ho, _____ let's pull to - geth - er now, boys. _____
The stars - 'll shine _____ a lit - tle bright - er than be - fore.

Gtr. 2

Gtr. 1

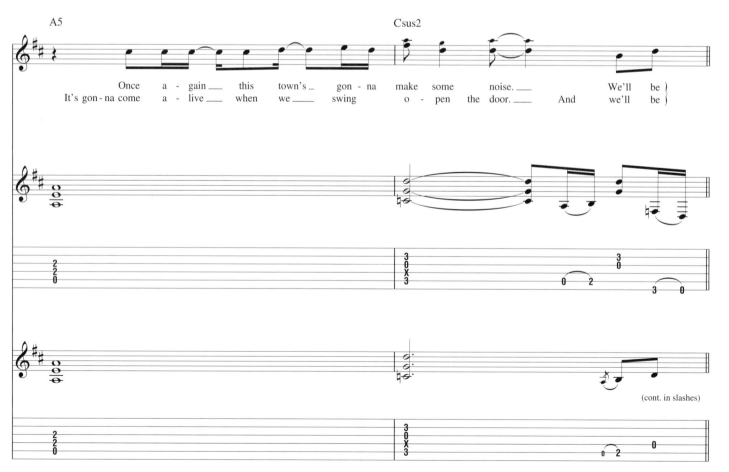

Once a - gain ___ this town's ___ gon - na make some noise. _____ We'll be }
It's gon - na come a - live ___ when we ___ swing o - pen the door. ___ And we'll be }

(cont. in slashes)

96

Verse

Gtrs. 1 & 2: w/ Rhy. Figs. 1 & 1A

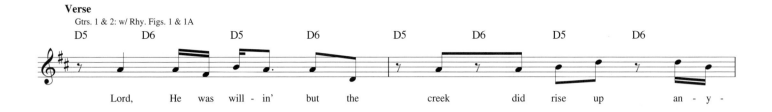

Lord, He was will - in' but the creek did rise up an - y -

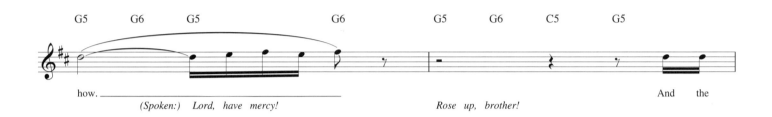

how. _____ (Spoken:) Lord, have mercy! Rose up, brother! And the

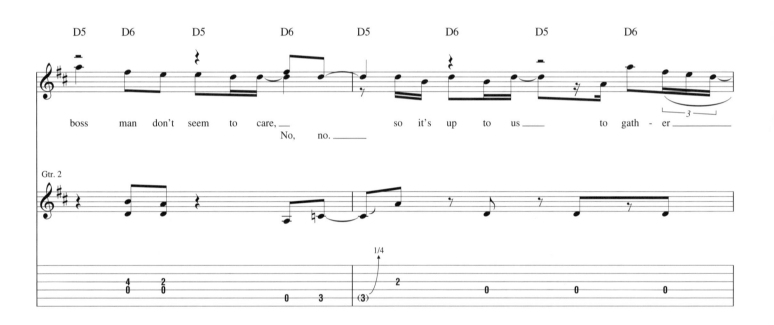

boss man don't seem to care, _____ so it's up to us _____ to gath - er
No, no. _____

Gtr. 2

D.S. al Coda 1

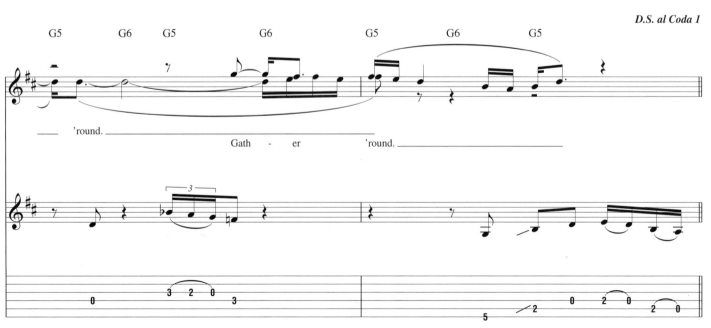

_____ 'round. _____ Gath - er 'round. _____

Coda 1

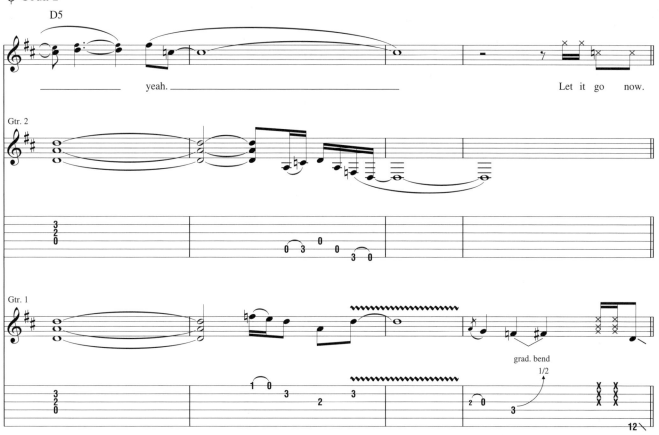

Interlude

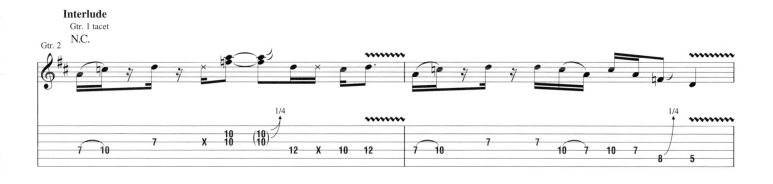

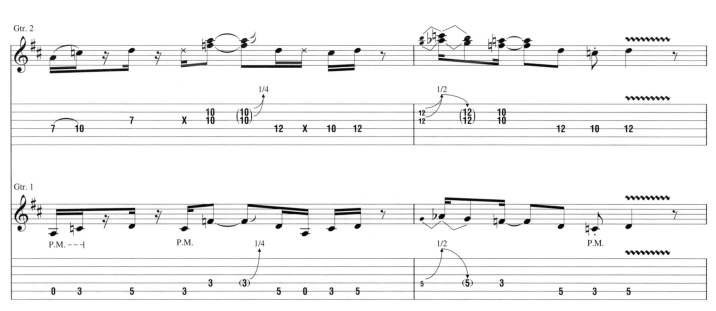

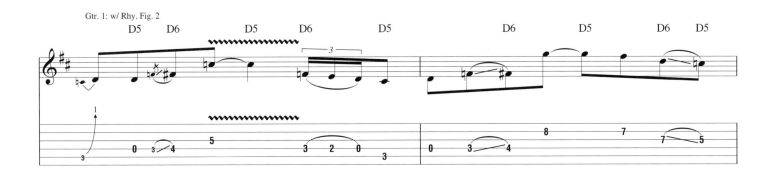

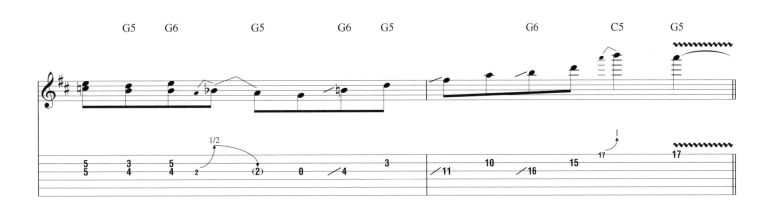

Pre-Chorus

So heave - ho, ___ let's pull to - geth - er now, boys. ___ Once a - gain ___ this town's ___ gon - na

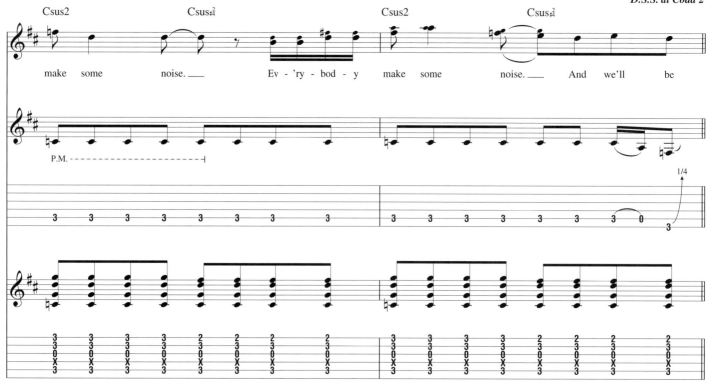

make some noise. ___ Ev - 'ry - bod - y make some noise. ___ And we'll be

Coda 2

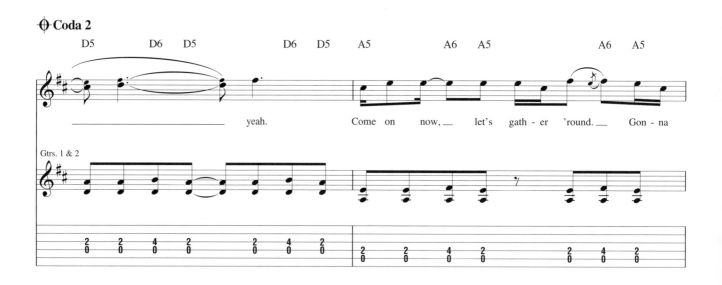

___ yeah. Come on now, ___ let's gath - er 'round. ___ Gon - na

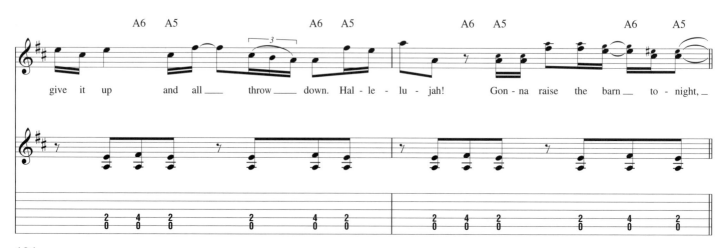

give it up and all ___ throw ___ down. Hal - le - lu - jah! Gon - na raise the barn ___ to - night, ___

God Made Woman

Words and Music by
Steve McEwan, Gordie Sampson
and Hillary Lindsey

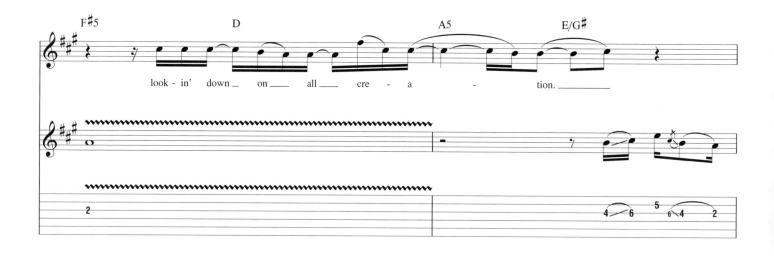

look - in' down _ on _ all _ cre - a - tion. _

He took a riv - er that winds _ and turns, He took a fi - re that breathes _ and burns _ and put it all _

D.S. al Coda

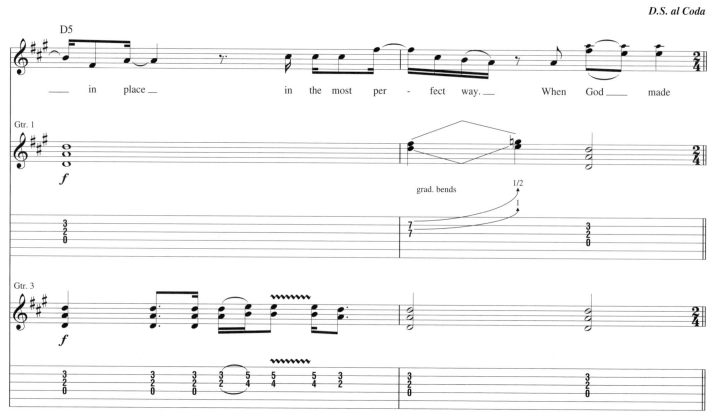

_ in place _ in the most per - fect way. _ When God _ made

110

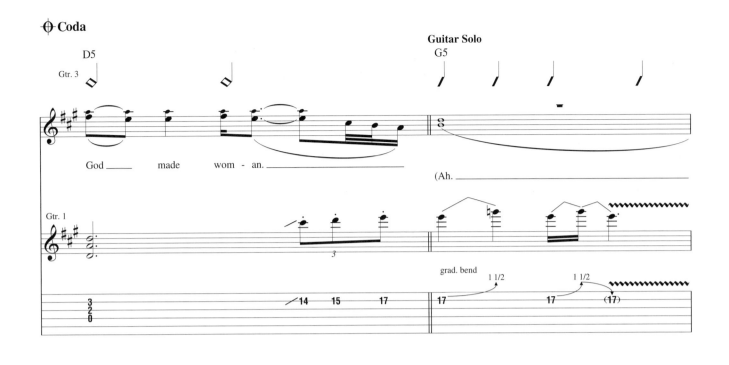

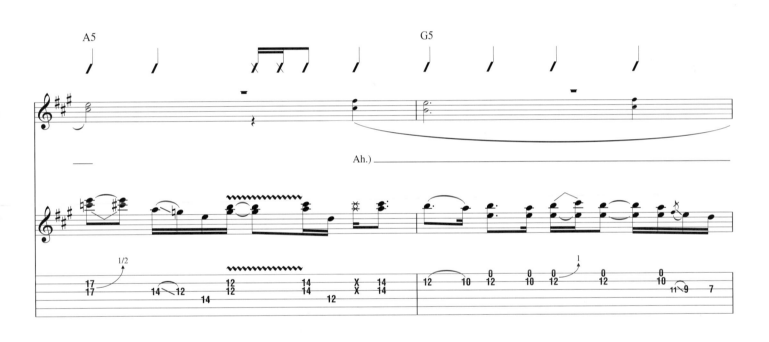

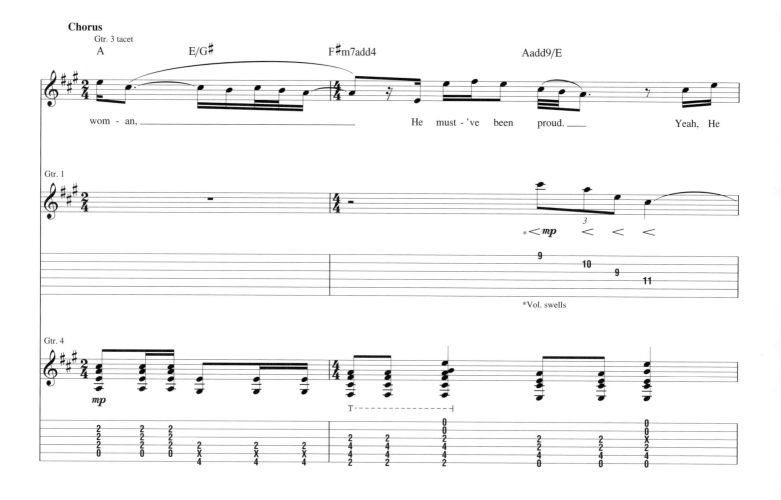

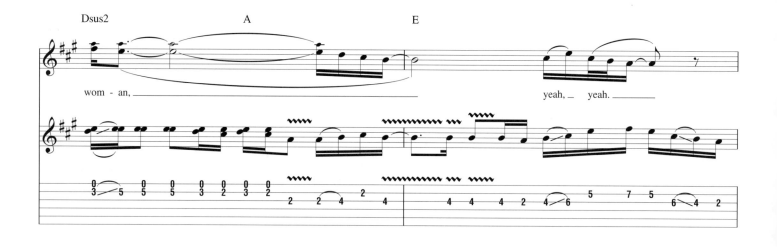

wom - an, _____ yeah, __ yeah. _____

Bkgd. Voc.: w/ Voc. Fig. 1

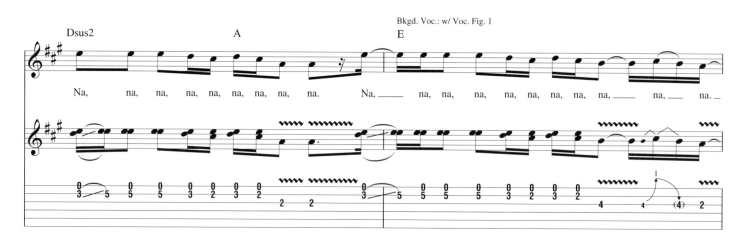

Na, na, na, na, na, na, na, na, na. Na, ___ na, na, na, na, na, na, na, na, ___ na, ___ na. _

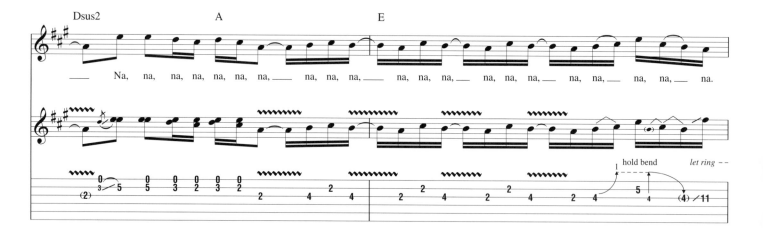

___ Na, na, na, na, na, na, na, ___ na, na, na, ___ na, na, na, ___ na, na, na, ___ na, na, ___ na, na, ___ na.

(Na, na, na, na, na, na, na, na, na. Na, ___ na, na, na, na, na, na, na, na.

*Refers to upstemmed voc. only.

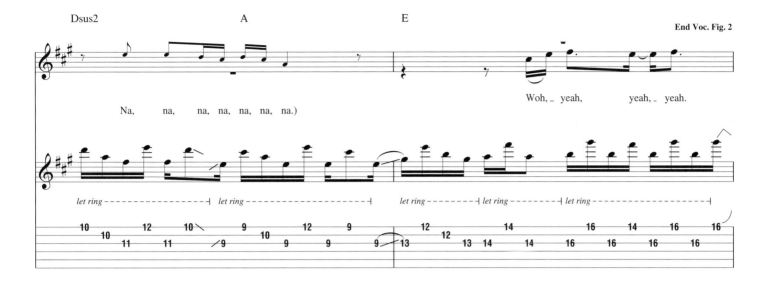

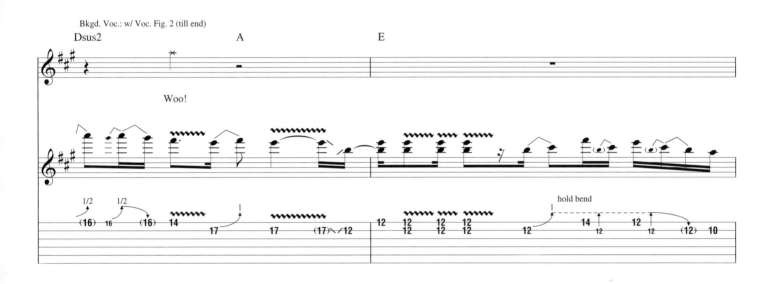

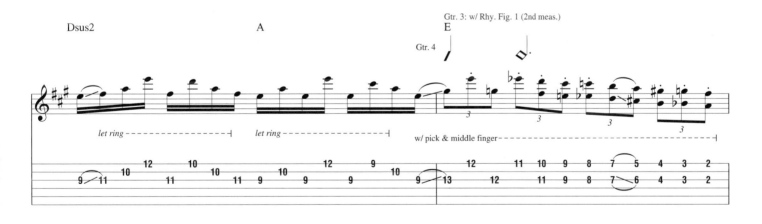

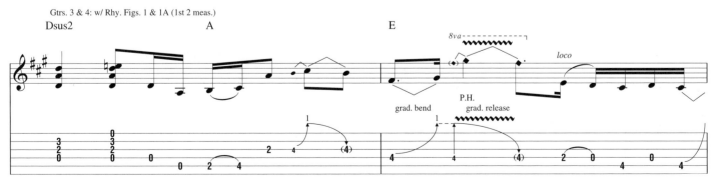

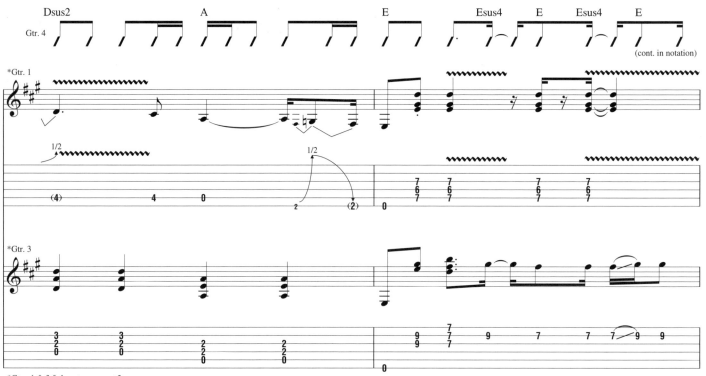

*Gtrs. 1 & 3 fade out over next 2 meas.

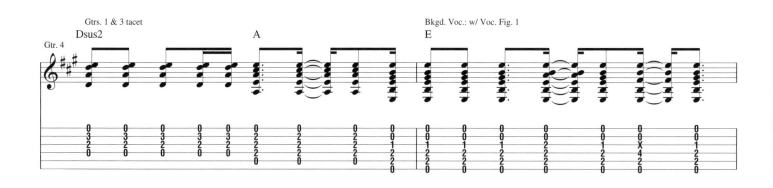

Tu Compañía

Words and Music by
Keith Urban and Monty Powell

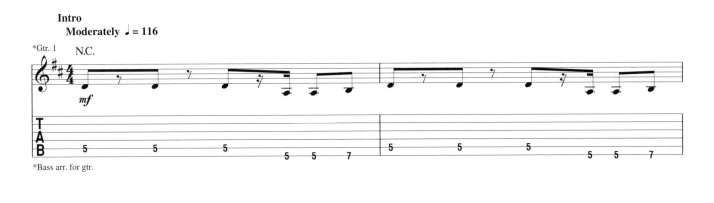

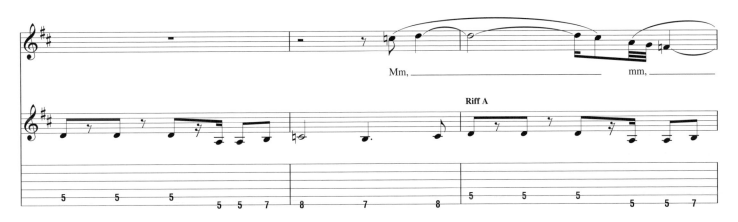

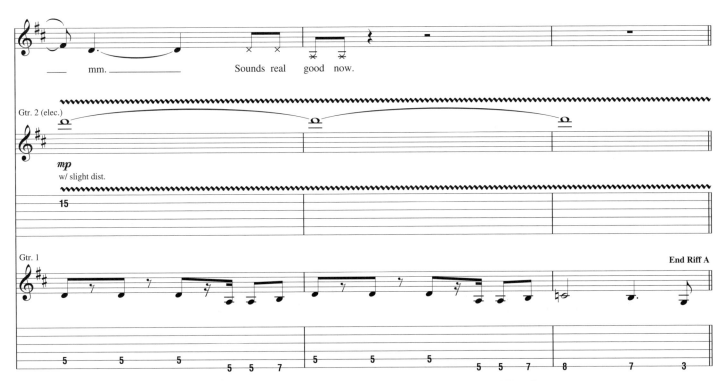

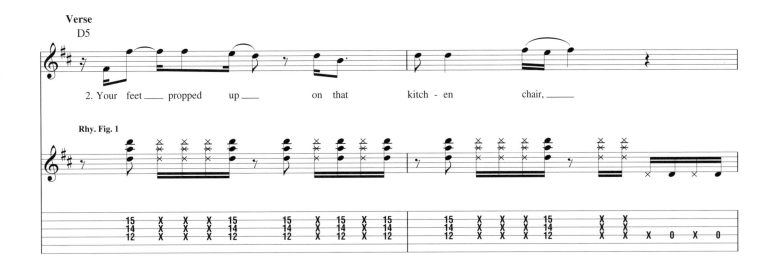

Verse

2. Your feet propped up on that kitch-en chair,

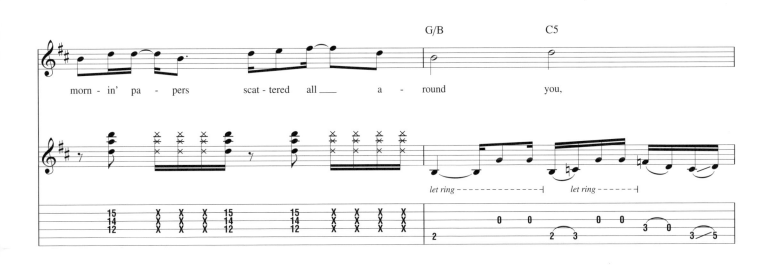

morn-in' pa-pers scat-tered all a-round you,

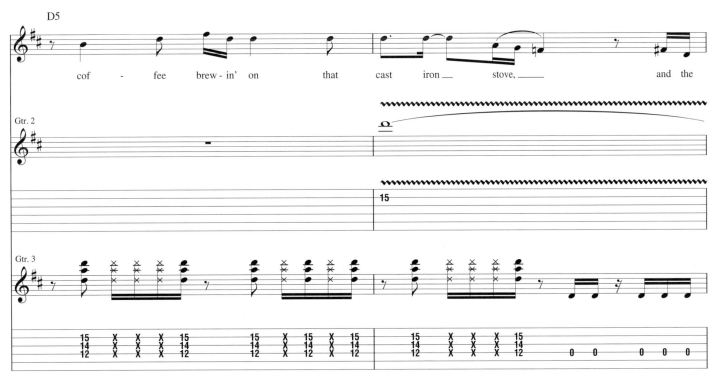

cof-fee brew-in' on that cast iron stove, and the

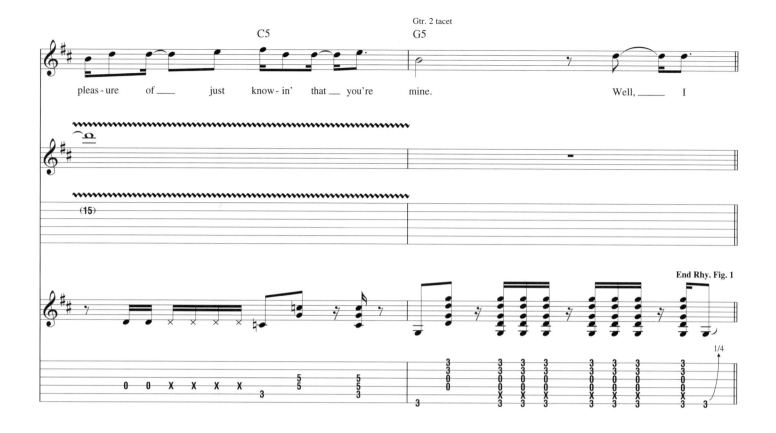

Chorus

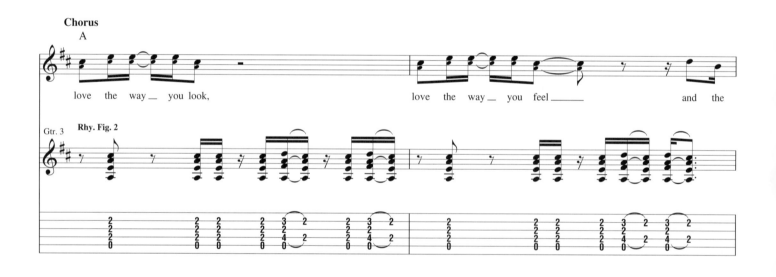

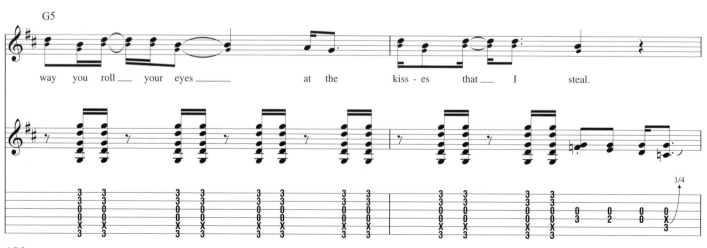

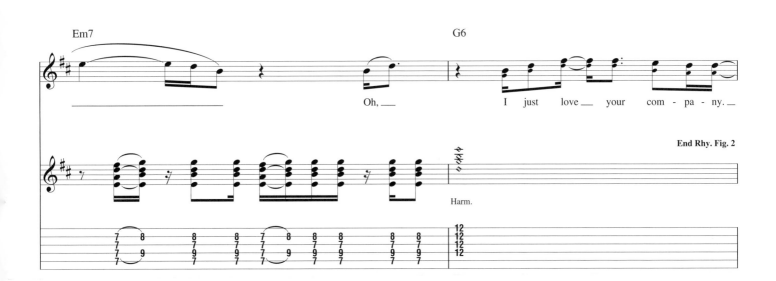

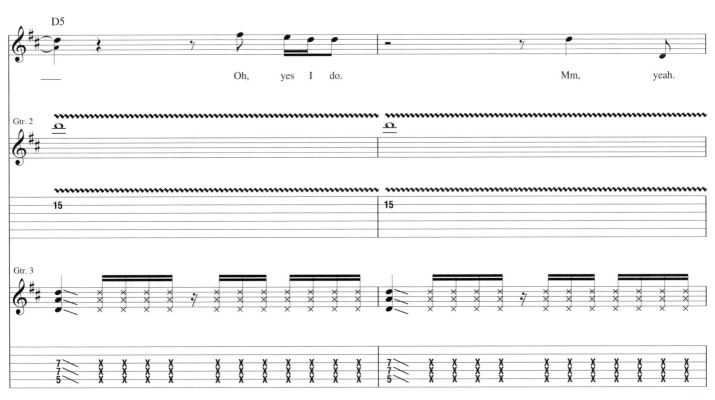

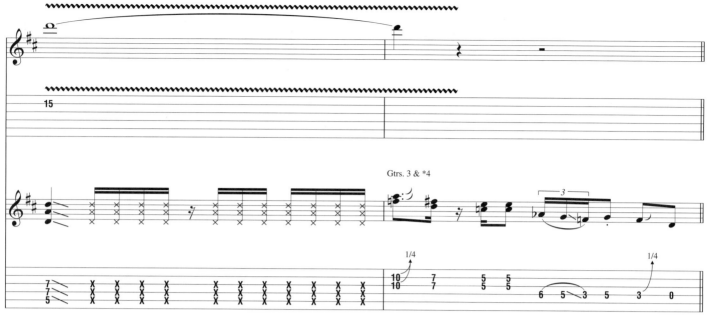

*Gtr. 4 (Ganjo): 6-string banjo tuned like a standard gtr.; *mf*.

Verse

Gtrs. 3 & 4: w/ Rhy. Fig. 1

3. Arm in arm ___ on some ___ spring ___ side - walk day, ___

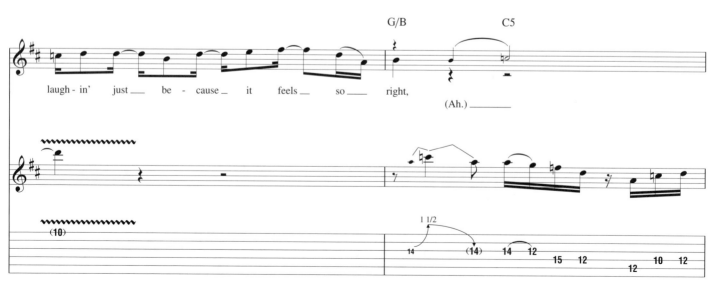

laugh - in' just ___ be - cause ___ it feels ___ so ___ right,

(Ah.) ___

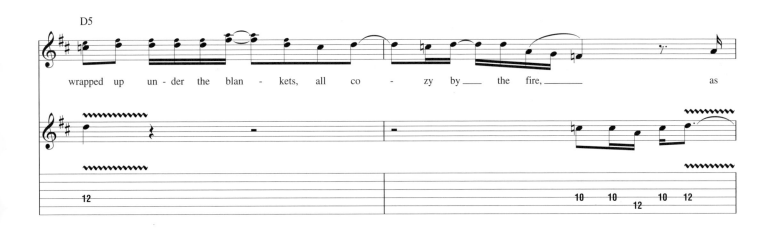

wrapped up un-der the blan - kets, all co - zy by __ the fire, _____ as

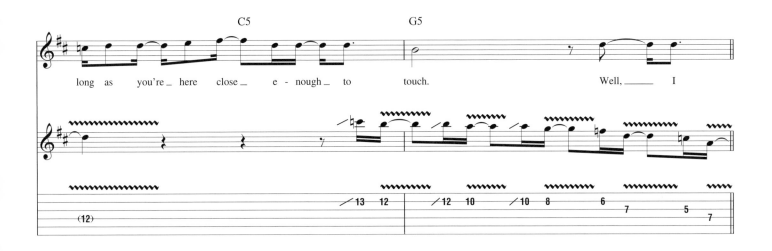

long as you're __ here close __ e - nough __ to touch. Well, _____ I

Chorus

Gtrs. 3 & 4: w/ Rhy. Fig. 2

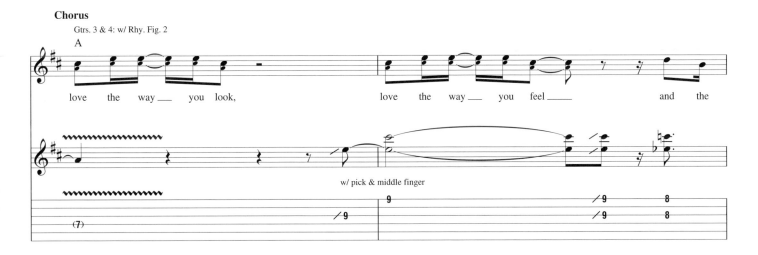

love the way __ you look, love the way __ you feel _____ and the

w/ pick & middle finger

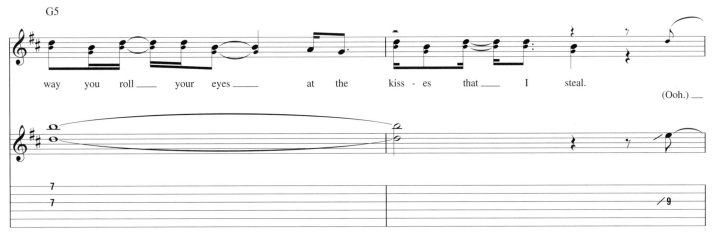

way you roll __ your eyes _____ at the kiss - es that ___ I steal.

(Ooh.) __

Love the way___ you stare___ when you're star - in' right at me.___

Interlude

Em7   G6 (Gtr. 2 tacet)   D

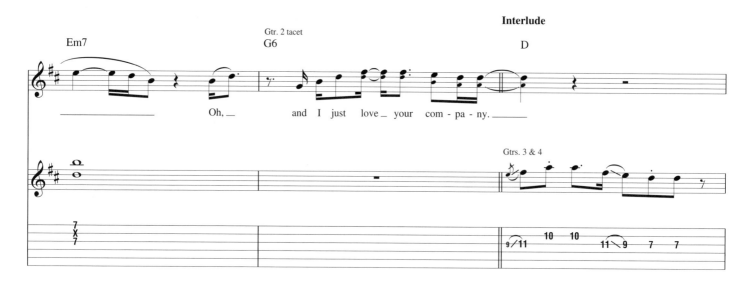

___ Oh,___ and I just love___ your com - pa - ny.___

Gtrs. 3 & 4

C/D   D   N.C.

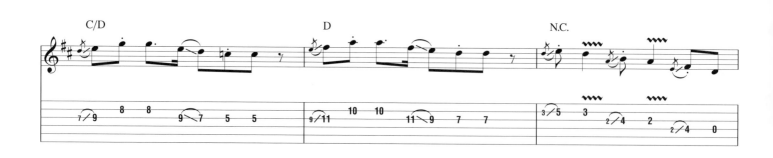

D   C/D

Doo doo doo doo___ doo doo.   Doo doo doo doo___ doo doo.

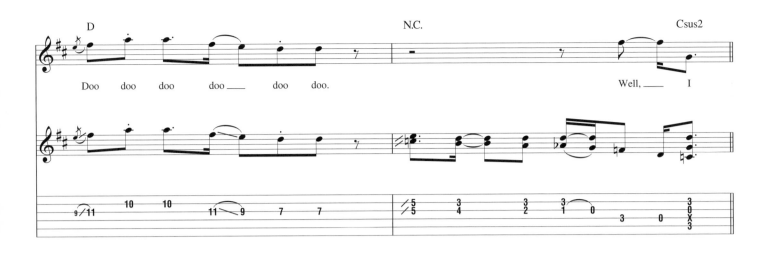

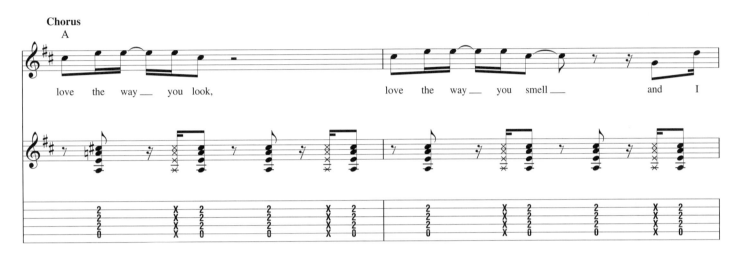

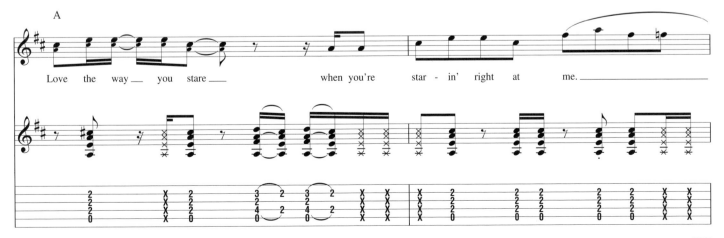

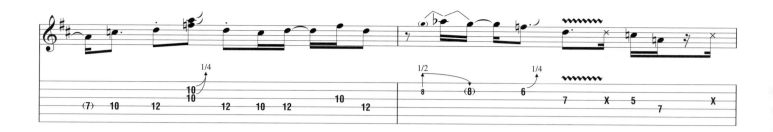

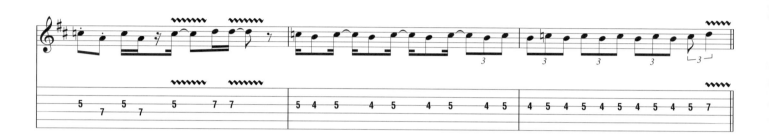

3rd time, Begin fade

Gtr. 2: w/ Riff C1 (3 times)
2nd & 3rd times, Gtr. 4: w/ Riff C

Doo doo doo doo ___ doo doo.   Doo doo doo doo ___ doo doo.

Doo doo doo doo ___ doo doo.   Doo da doo da doo da.

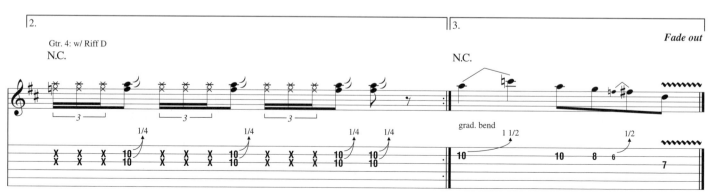

Gtr. 4: w/ Riff D

Fade out

Everybody

Words and Music by
Keith Urban and Richard Marx

Verse

Gtr. 1: w/ Rhy. Fig. 1 (3 1/4 times)
Gtr. 2 tacet

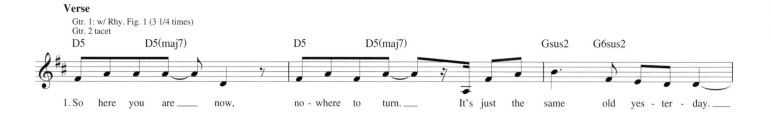

1. So here you are now, no - where to turn. It's just the same old yes - ter - day.

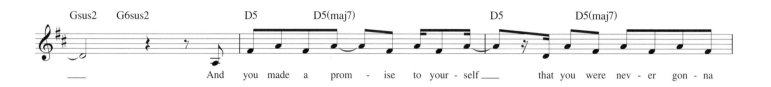

And you made a prom - ise to your - self that you were nev - er gon - na

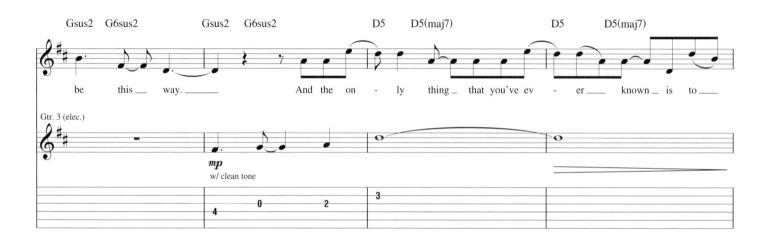

be this way. And the on - ly thing that you've ev - er known is to

Gtr. 3 (elec.)

mp
w/ clean tone

Gtr. 3 tacet

run. So you keep on driv - in' fast -

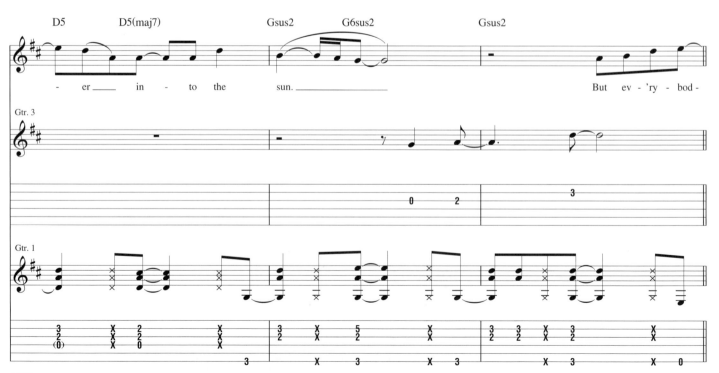

- er in - to the sun. But ev - 'ry - bod -

Gtr. 3

Gtr. 1

Chorus

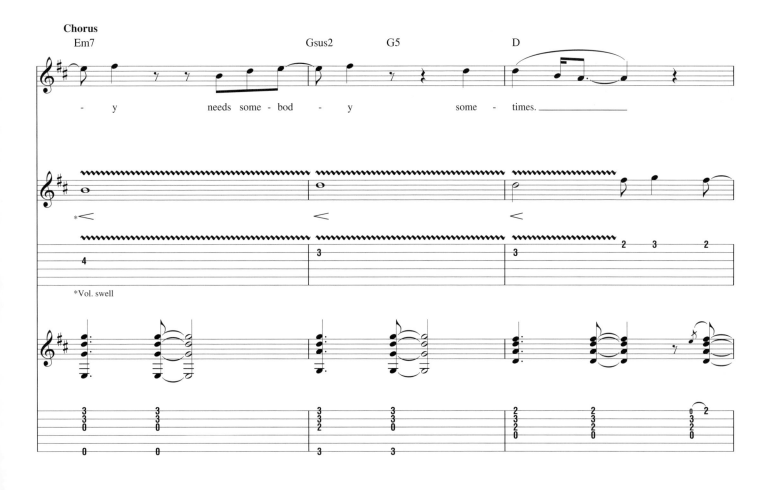

- y   needs some - bod - y   some - times. _____

*Vol. swell

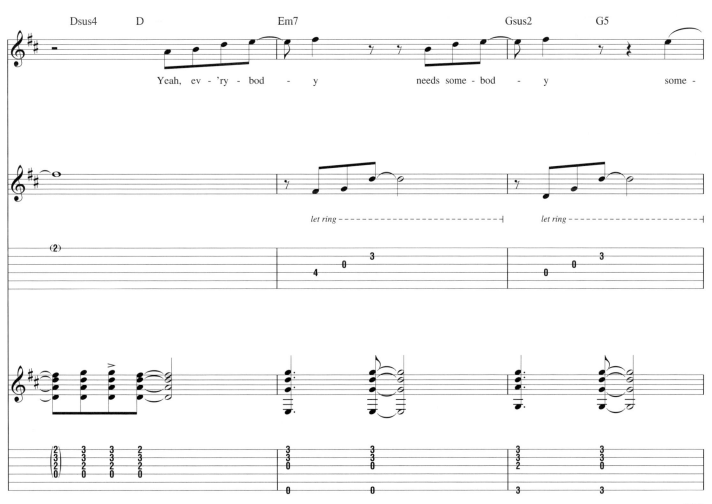

Yeah, ev - 'ry - bod - y   needs some - bod - y   some -

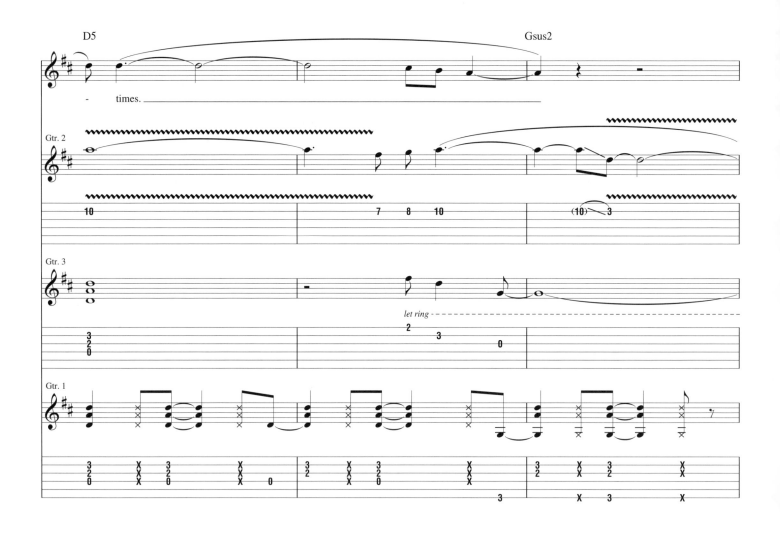

Verse

Gtr. 1: w/ Rhy. Fig. 1 (2 1/2 times)
Gtr. 2 tacet

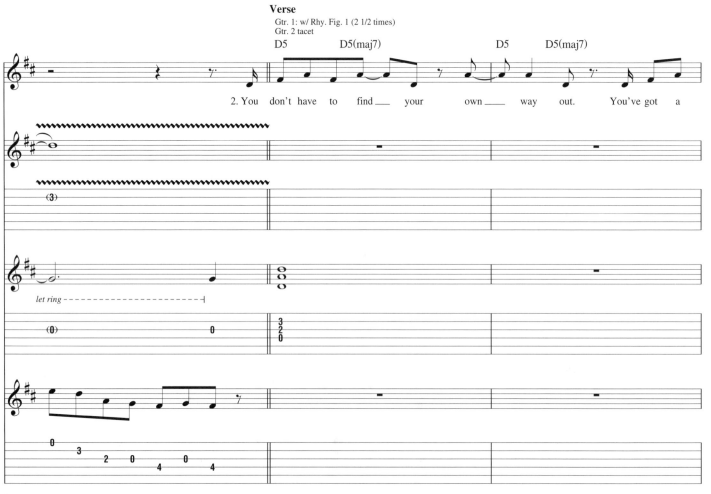

2. You don't have to find ___ your own ___ way out. You've got a

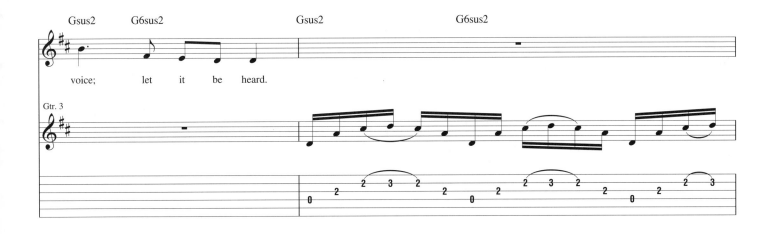

voice; let it be heard.

Just when it feels _____ you're on a dead - end road, _____ there's al - ways

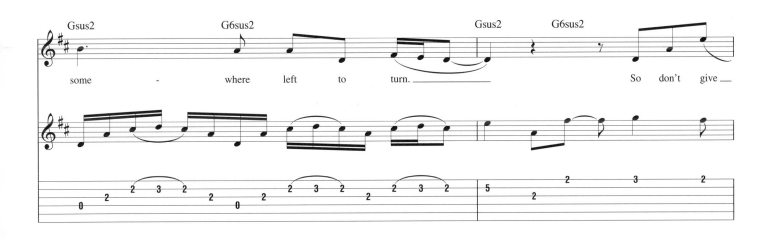

some - where left to turn. _____ So don't give _____

_____ up now. _____ You're so close _____ to a brand - new
(Don't give _____ up now.) _____

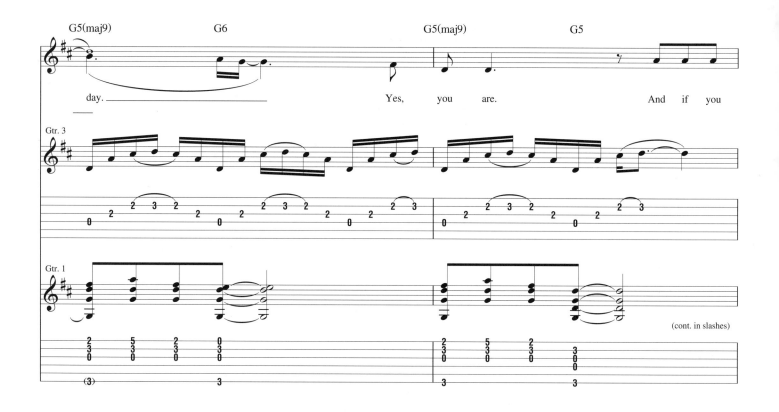

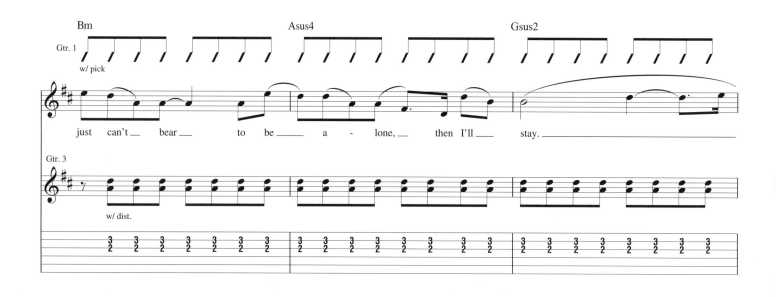

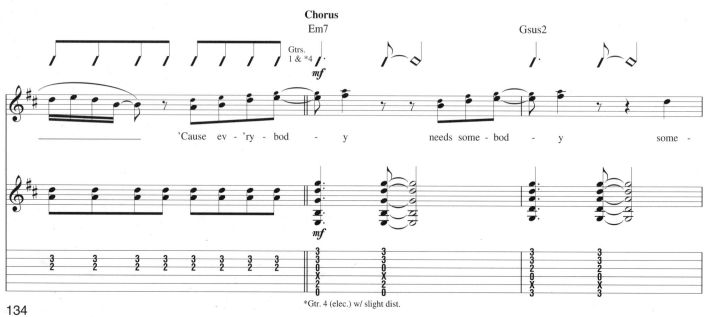

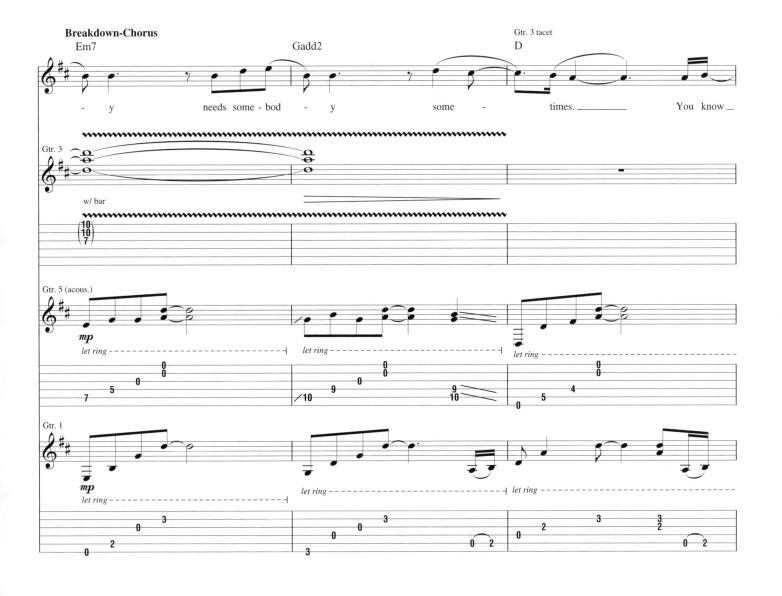

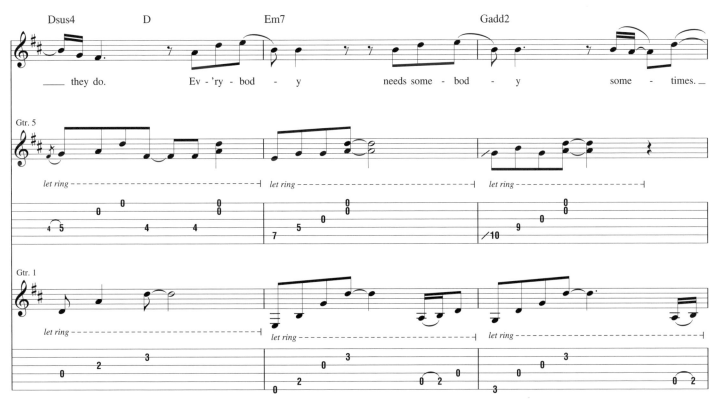

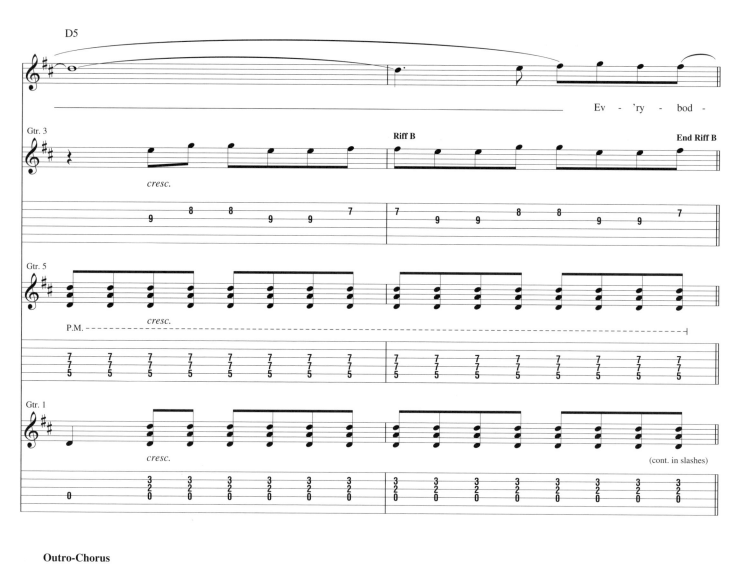

Outro-Chorus

Gtr. 3: w/ Riff B (12 times)
Gtr. 5 tacet

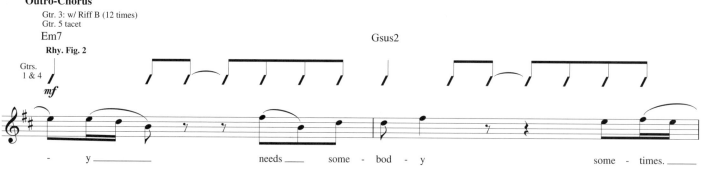

- y _____ needs _____ some - bod - y _____ some - times. _____

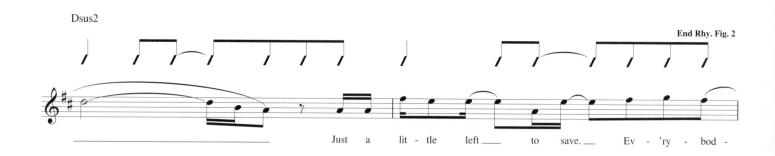

_____ Just a lit - tle left _____ to save. _____ Ev - 'ry - bod-

Gtrs. 1 & 4: w/ Rhy. Fig. 2 (2 times)

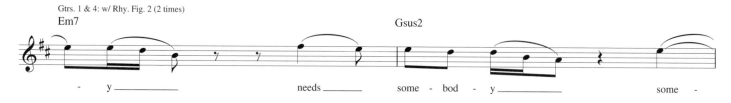

- y _____ needs _____ some - bod - y _____ some -

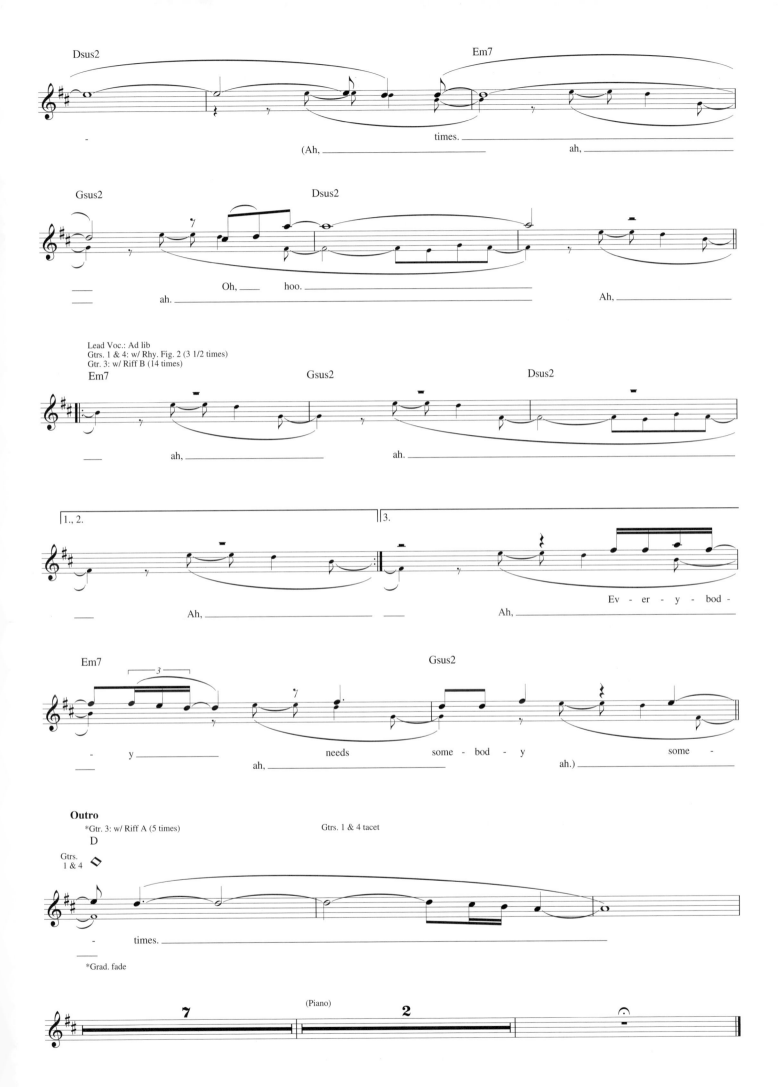

Got It Right This Time

Words and Music by
Keith Urban

140

Bridge

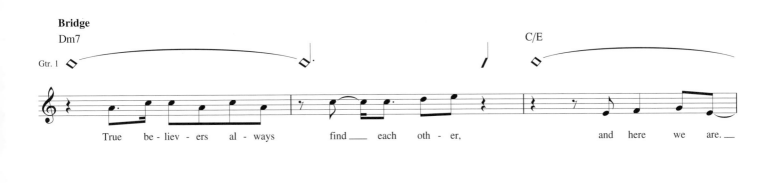

True be-liev-ers al-ways find each oth-er, and here we are.

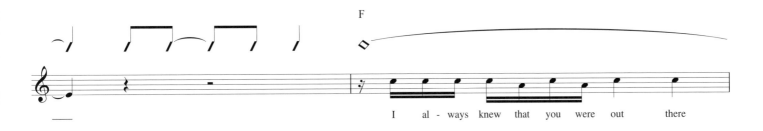

I al-ways knew that you were out there

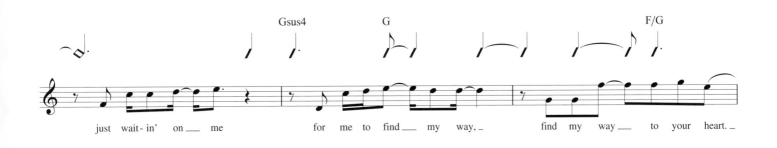

just wait-in' on me for me to find my way, find my way to your heart.

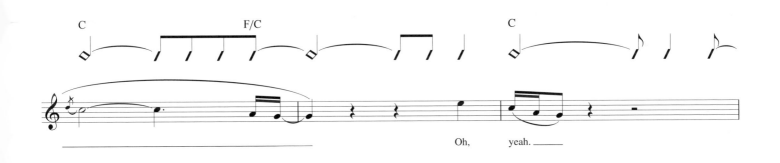

Oh, yeah.

Chorus

Gtr. 1: w/ Rhy. Fig. 2

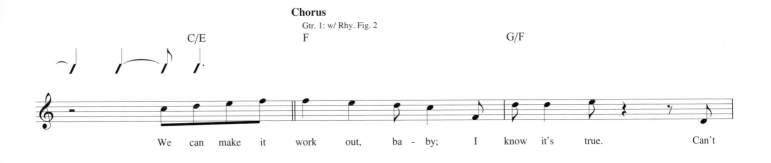

We can make it work out, ba-by; I know it's true. Can't

pic-ture my-self with no one but you. And I think I got it right

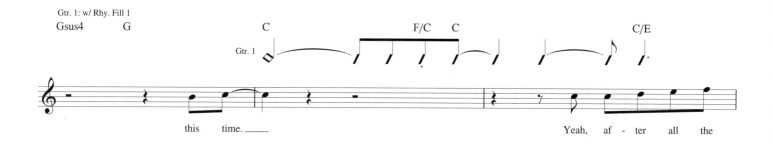

this time. _____ Yeah, af - ter all the

cra - zy days _____ I made it through, I can't pic - ture my - self with

no one but you. _____ And I think I got it right _____ this time. _

_____ Oh, yeah. _____

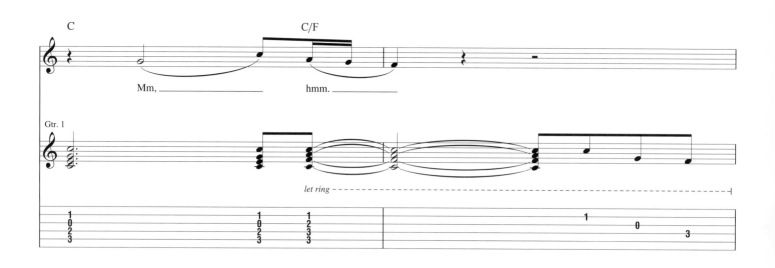

Mm, _____ hmm. _____

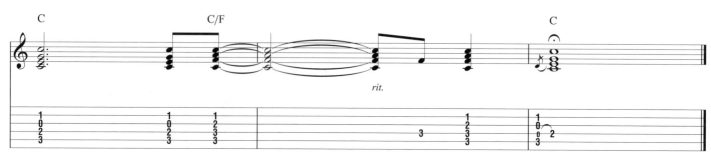

Slow Turning

Words and Music by
John Hiatt

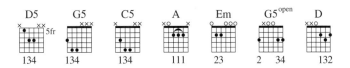

Gtrs. 1-5: Tune down 1 step:
(low to high) D-G-C-F-A-D
Gtr. 6: Drop D tuning, down 1 step:
(low to high) C-G-C-F-A-D

Intro

Moderately fast ♩ = 140

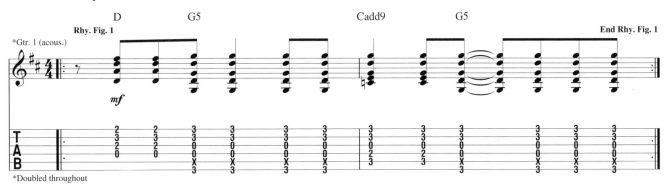

*Gtr. 1 (acous.)

*Doubled throughout

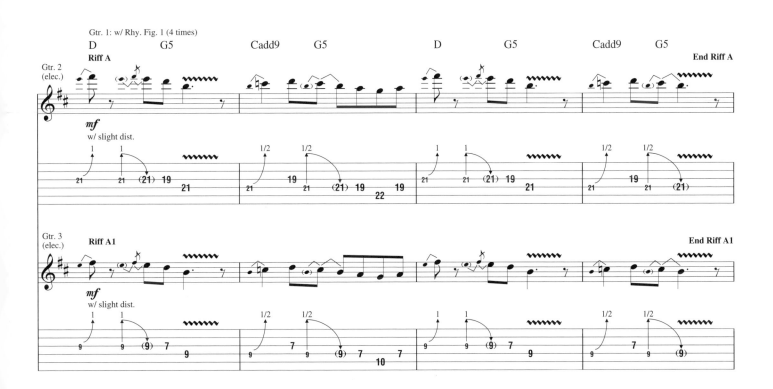

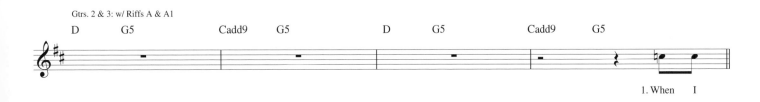

1. When   I

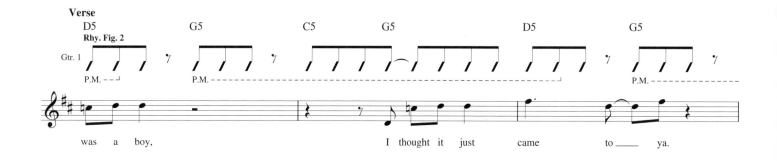

was a boy, I thought it just came to ___ ya.

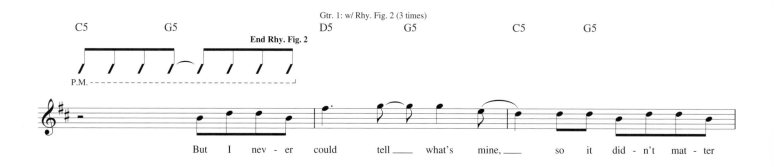

But I nev-er could tell ___ what's mine, ___ so it did-n't mat-ter

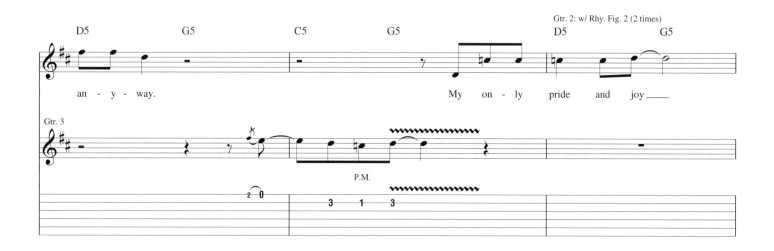

an - y - way. My on - ly pride and joy ___

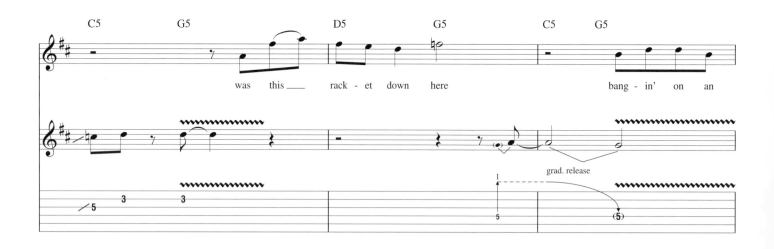

was this ___ rack-et down here bang-in' on an

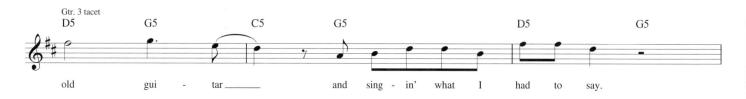

old gui-tar ___ and sing-in' what I had to say.

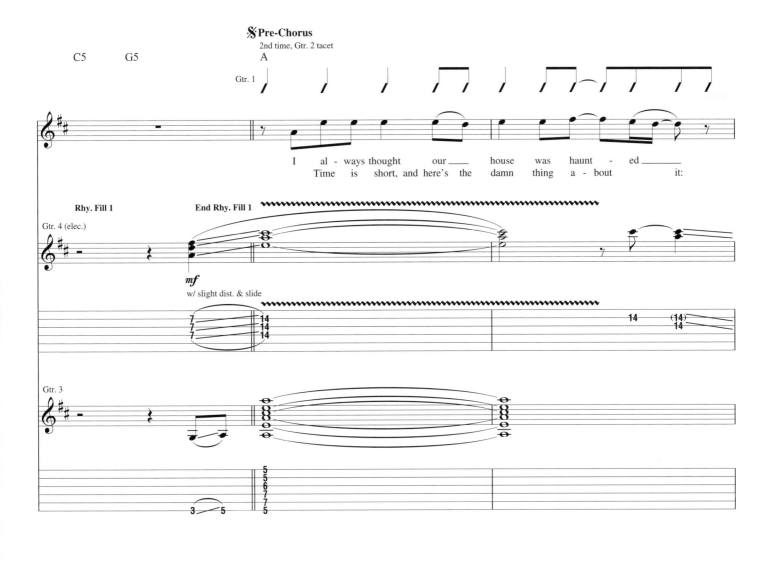

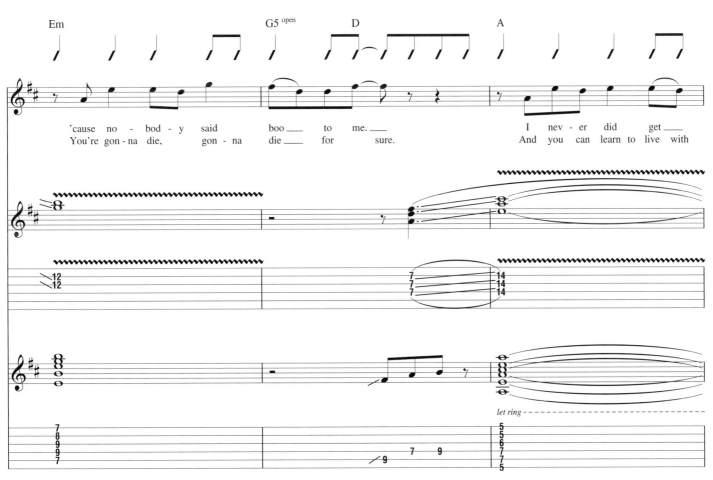

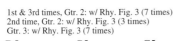

1st & 3rd times, Gtr. 2: w/ Rhy. Fig. 3 (7 times)
2nd time, Gtr. 2: w/ Rhy. Fig. 3 (3 times)
Gtr. 3: w/ Rhy. Fig. 3 (7 times)

out.　A slow turn - in' _____ but you come { (1.) a -
                                              { (2., 3.) a -

2nd time, Gtr. 2: w/ Riff B (4 times)

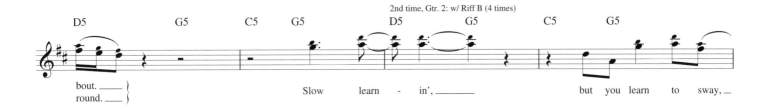

bout. ___ }
round. ___ }　Slow learn - in', _____ but you learn to sway, ___

To Coda 1

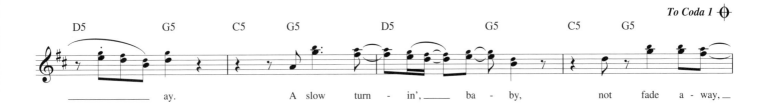

_____ ay.　A slow turn - in', ___ ba - by, not fade a - way, ___

To Coda 2 **Interlude**

Gtr. 1: w/ Rhy. Fig. 1 (2 times)
Gtrs. 2 & 3: w/ Riffs A & A1

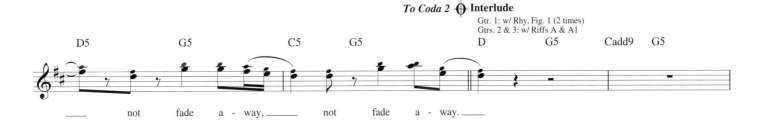

___ not fade a - way, _____ not fade a - way. ___

Verse

Gtrs. 1 & 2: w/ Rhy. Fig. 2 (1 3/4 times)

2. Now I'm in my car; ___ I got the

ra - di - o down.　And I'm yell - in' at the kids in the

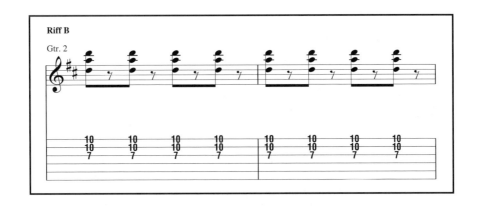

149

back 'cause they're bang - in' like Char - lie Watts.

You think you've come so far in this ___

one - horse town. Then she's ___ laugh - in' that cra - zy laugh ___

___ 'cause you have - n't left the park - in' lot.

150

⊕ Coda 1

D5   G5   C5   G5

____   not   fade   a - way. ____   There's   just   a   slow   turn -

⊕ Coda 2

Gtr. 1: w/ Rhy. Fig. 1 (8 times)
Gtrs. 2 & 3: w/ Riffs A & A1 (4 times)
Gtr. 6: w/ Riff C (8 times)

Lead Voc.: Ad lib

*Fretboard position located halfway
between 21st and 22nd frets.

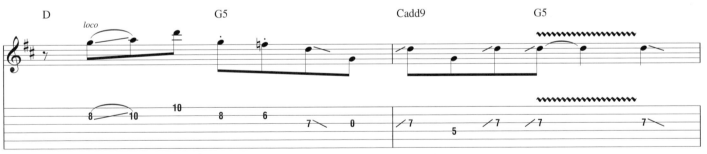

Riff C

Gtr. 6 (**Ganjo)

mf

let ring

**6-string banjo tuned as indicated on first page of song.

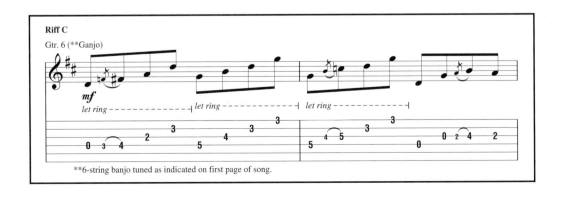

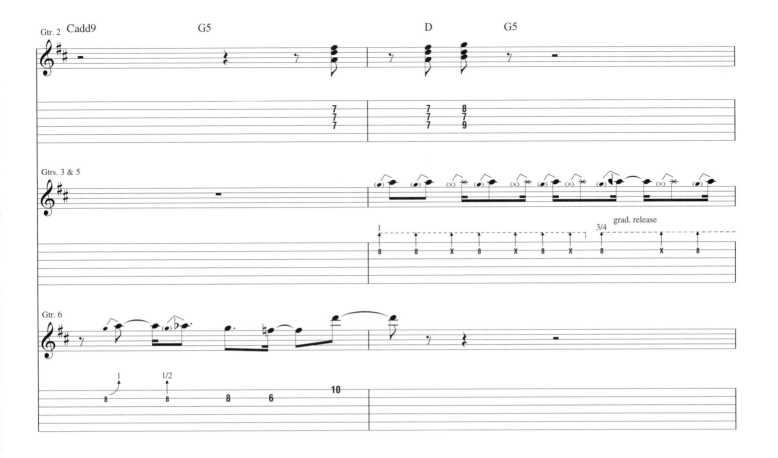

Outro-Guitar Solo
Gtr. 1: w/ Rhy. Fig. 1 (16 times)
Gtrs. 2 & 3: w/ Rhy. Fig. 3 (16 times)
Gtr. 6: w/ Riff C (16 times)

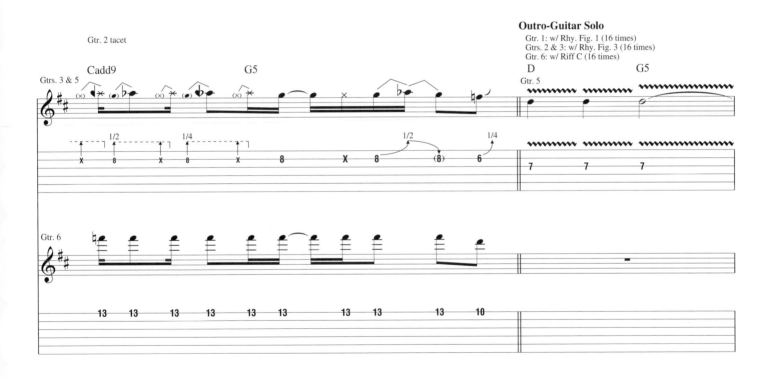

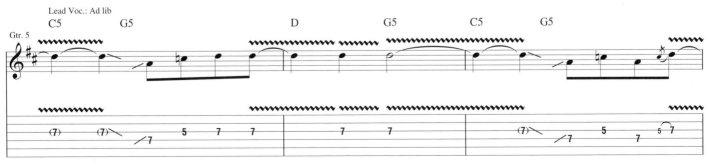

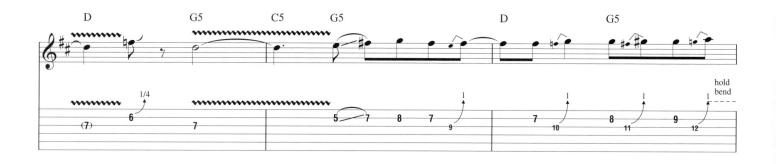

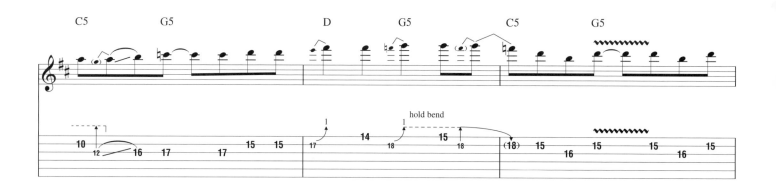

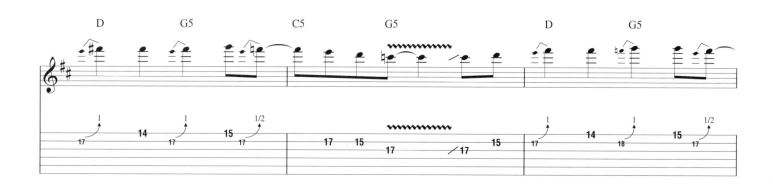

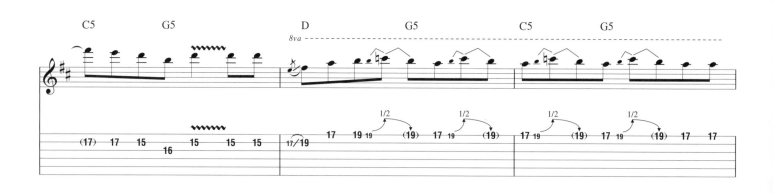

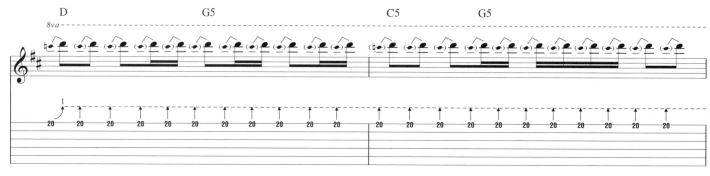

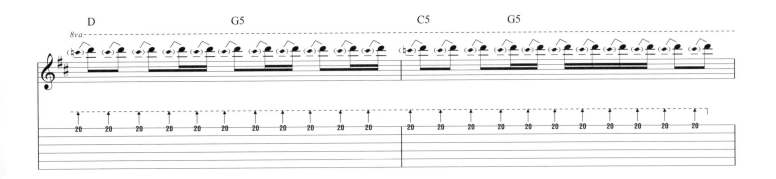

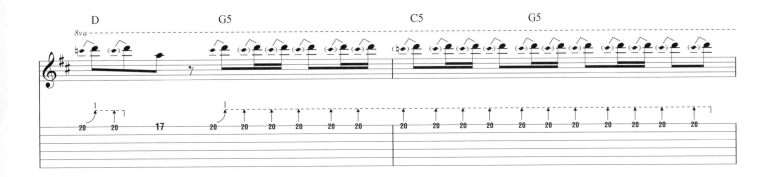

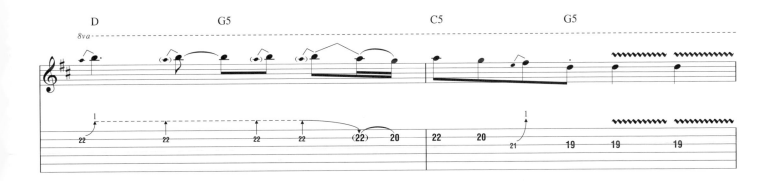

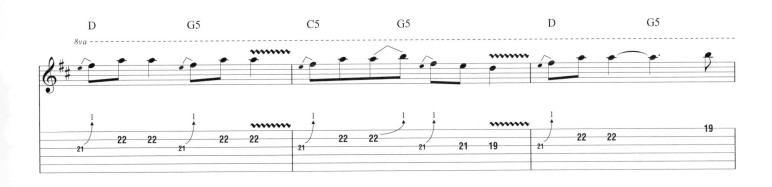

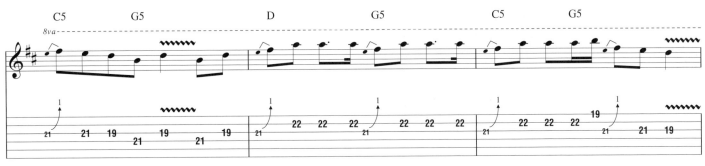

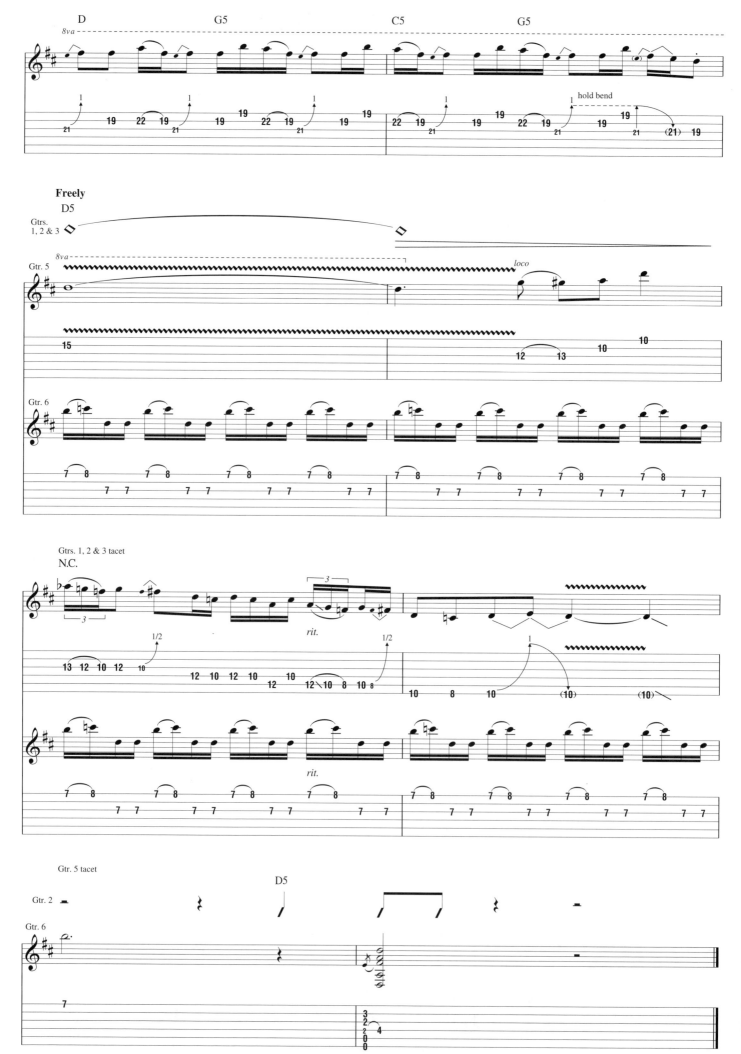

Guitar Notation Legend

Guitar music can be notated three different ways: on a *musical staff*, in *tablature*, and in *rhythm slashes*.

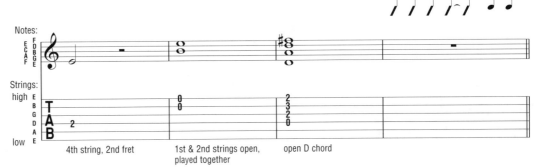

RHYTHM SLASHES are written above the staff. Strum chords in the rhythm indicated. Use the chord diagrams found at the top of the first page of the transcription for the appropriate chord voicings. Round noteheads indicate single notes.

THE MUSICAL STAFF shows pitches and rhythms and is divided by bar lines into measures. Pitches are named after the first seven letters of the alphabet.

TABLATURE graphically represents the guitar fingerboard. Each horizontal line represents a string, and each number represents a fret.

HALF-STEP BEND: Strike the note and bend up 1/2 step.

BEND AND RELEASE: Strike the note and bend up as indicated, then release back to the original note. Only the first note is struck.

HAMMER-ON: Strike the first (lower) note with one finger, then sound the higher note (on the same string) with another finger by fretting it without picking.

TRILL: Very rapidly alternate between the notes indicated by continuously hammering on and pulling off.

PICK SCRAPE: The edge of the pick is rubbed down (or up) the string, producing a scratchy sound.

TREMOLO PICKING: The note is picked as rapidly and continuously as possible.

WHOLE-STEP BEND: Strike the note and bend up one step.

PRE-BEND: Bend the note as indicated, then strike it.

PULL-OFF: Place both fingers on the notes to be sounded. Strike the first note and without picking, pull the finger off to sound the second (lower) note.

TAPPING: Hammer ("tap") the fret indicated with the pick-hand index or middle finger and pull off to the note fretted by the fret hand.

MUFFLED STRINGS: A percussive sound is produced by laying the fret hand across the string(s) without depressing, and striking them with the pick hand.

VIBRATO BAR DIVE AND RETURN: The pitch of the note or chord is dropped a specified number of steps (in rhythm), then returned to the original pitch.

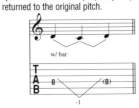

GRACE NOTE BEND: Strike the note and immediately bend up as indicated.

VIBRATO: The string is vibrated by rapidly bending and releasing the note with the fretting hand.

LEGATO SLIDE: Strike the first note and then slide the same fret-hand finger up or down to the second note. The second note is not struck.

NATURAL HARMONIC: Strike the note while the fret-hand lightly touches the string directly over the fret indicated.

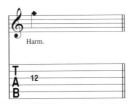

PALM MUTING: The note is partially muted by the pick hand lightly touching the string(s) just before the bridge.

VIBRATO BAR SCOOP: Depress the bar just before striking the note, then quickly release the bar.

SLIGHT (MICROTONE) BEND: Strike the note and bend up 1/4 step.

WIDE VIBRATO: The pitch is varied to a greater degree by vibrating with the fretting hand.

SHIFT SLIDE: Same as legato slide, except the second note is struck.

PINCH HARMONIC: The note is fretted normally and a harmonic is produced by adding the edge of the thumb or the tip of the index finger of the pick hand to the normal pick attack.

RAKE: Drag the pick across the strings indicated with a single motion.

VIBRATO BAR DIP: Strike the note and then immediately drop a specified number of steps, then release back to the original pitch.

157

CHERRY LANE MUSIC COMPANY

6 East 32nd Street, New York, NY 10016

Quality in Printed Music

The Magazine You Can Play

Visit the Guitar One web site at **www.guitarone.com**

ACOUSTIC INSTRUMENTALISTS

INCLUDES TAB

Over 15 transcriptions from legendary artists such as Leo Kottke, John Fahey, Jorma Kaukonen, Chet Atkins, Adrian Legg, Jeff Beck, and more.

02500399 Play-It-Like-It-Is Guitar............................$9.95

THE BEST BASS LINES

INCLUDES TAB

24 super songs: Bohemian Rhapsody • Celebrity Skin • Crash Into Me • Crazy Train • Glycerine • Money • November Rain • Smoke on the Water • Sweet Child O' Mine • What Would You Say • You're My Flavor • and more.

02500311 Play-It-Like-It-Is Bass $14.95

BLUES TAB

INCLUDES TAB

14 songs: Boom Boom • Cold Shot • Hide Away • I Can't Quit You Baby • I'm Your Hoochie Coochie Man • In 2 Deep • It Hurts Me Too • Talk to Your Daughter • The Thrill Is Gone • and more.

02500410 Play-It-Like-It-Is Guitar..........................$14.95

CLASSIC ROCK TAB

INCLUDES TAB

15 rock hits: Cat Scratch Fever • Crazy Train • Day Tripper • Hey Joe • Hot Blooded • Start Me Up • We Will Rock You • You Really Got Me • and more.

02500408 Play-It-Like-It-Is Guitar..........................$14.95

MODERN ROCK TAB

INCLUDES TAB

15 of modern rock's best: Are You Gonna Go My Way • Denial • Hanging by a Moment • I Did It • My Hero • Nobody's Real • Rock the Party (Off the Hook) • Shock the Monkey • Slide • Spit It Out • and more.

02500409 Play-It-Like-It-Is Guitar..........................$14.95

SIGNATURE SONGS

INCLUDES TAB

21 artists' trademark hits: Crazy Train (Ozzy Osbourne) • My Generation (The Who) • Smooth (Santana) • Sunshine of Your Love (Cream) • Walk This Way (Aerosmith) • Welcome to the Jungle (Guns N' Roses) • What Would You Say (Dave Matthews Band) • and more.

02500303 Play-It-Like-It-Is Guitar..........................$16.95

BASS SECRETS

WHERE TODAY'S BASS STYLISTS GET TO THE BOTTOM LINE
compiled by John Stix

Bass Secrets brings together 48 columns highlighting specific topics – ranging from the technical to the philosophical – from masters such as Stu Hamm, Randy Coven, Tony Franklin and Billy Sheehan. They cover topics including tapping, walking bass lines, soloing, hand positions, harmonics and more. Clearly illustrated with musical examples.

02500100 ....$12.95

CLASSICS ILLUSTRATED

WHERE BACH MEETS ROCK
by Robert Phillips

Classics Illustrated is designed to demonstrate for readers and players the links between rock and classical music. Each of the 30 columns from *Guitar* highlights one musical concept and provides clear examples in both styles of music. This cool book lets you study moving bass lines over stationary chords in the music of Bach and Guns N' Roses, learn the similarities between "Leyenda" and "Diary of a Madman," and much more!

02500101 ....$9.95

GUITAR SECRETS

INCLUDES TAB

WHERE ROCK'S GUITAR MASTERS SHARE THEIR TRICKS, TIPS & TECHNIQUES
compiled by John Stix

This unique and informative compilation features 42 columns culled from *Guitar* magazine. Readers will discover dozens of techniques and playing tips, and gain practical advice and words of wisdom from guitar masters.

02500099 ....$10.95

IN THE LISTENING ROOM

WHERE ARTISTS CRITIQUE THE MUSIC OF THEIR PEERS
compiled by John Stix

A compilation of 75 columns from *Guitar* magazine, *In the Listening Room* provides a unique opportunity for readers to hear major recording artists remark on the music of their peers. These artists were given no information about what they would hear, and their comments often tell as much about themselves as they do about the music they listened to. Includes candid critiques by music legends like Aerosmith, Jeff Beck, Jack Bruce, Dimebag Darrell, Buddy Guy, Kirk Hammett, Eric Johnson, John McLaughlin, Dave Navarro, Carlos Santana, Joe Satriani, Stevie Ray Vaughan, and many others.

02500097 ....$14.95

LEGENDS OF LEAD GUITAR

THE BEST OF INTERVIEWS: 1995-2000

This is a fascinating compilation of interviews with today's greatest guitarists! From deeply rooted blues giants to the most fearless pioneers, legendary players reveal how they achieve their extraordinary craft.

02500329 ....$14.95

LESSON LAB

This exceptional book/CD pack features more than 20 in-depth lessons. Tackle in detail a variety of pertinent music- and guitar-related subjects, such as scales, chords, theory, guitar technique, songwriting, and much more!

02500330 Book/CD Pack.......................................$19.95

NOISE & FEEDBACK

THE BEST OF 1995-2000: YOUR QUESTIONS ANSWERED

If you ever wanted to know about a specific guitar lick, trick, technique or effect, this book/CD pack is for you! It features over 70 lessons on composing • computer assistance • education and career advice • equipment • technique • terminology and notation • tunings • and more.

02500328 Book/CD Pack.......................................$17.95

OPEN EARS

A JOURNEY THROUGH LIFE WITH GUITAR IN HAND
by Steve Morse

In this collection of 50 *Guitar* magazine columns from the mid-'90s on, guitarist Steve Morse sets the story straight about what being a working musician *really* means. He deals out practical advice on: playing with the band, songwriting, recording and equipment, and more, through anecdotes of his hard-knock lessons learned.

02500333 ....$10.95

SPOTLIGHT ON STYLE

THE BEST OF 1995-2000: AN EXPLORER'S GUIDE TO GUITAR

This book and CD cover 18 of the world's most popular guitar styles, including: blues guitar • classical guitar • country guitar • funk guitar • jazz guitar • Latin guitar • metal • rockabilly and more!

02500320 Book/CD Pack.......................................$19.95

STUDIO CITY

PROFESSIONAL SESSION RECORDING FOR GUITARISTS
by Carl Verheyen

In this collection of colomns from Guitar Magazine, guitarists will learn how to: exercise studio etiquette and act professionally • acquire, assemble and set up gear for sessions • use the tricks of the trade to become a studio hero • get repeat call-backs • and more.

02500195 ....$9.95